THE MILES WE CHASE

BUILDING A FUTURE OF BELONGING IN EDUCATION AND LIFE

LOC H. NGUYEN

BY LOC H. NGUYEN

This is the author's first book, offered with gratitude and hope.

THE MILES WE CHASE

THE MILES WE CHASE

BUILDING A FUTURE OF BELONGING IN EDUCATION AND LIFE

LOC H. NGUYEN

Published by Bayhaus Press

San Francisco, California

ISBN: 979-8-218-78088-3

Cover design by Bayhaus Creative

Interior Design by Vellum

Printed in the United States of America

First Edition

For JR because you never had the chance to see this world.

CONTENTS

	Prologue	1
1.	The Hopes and Dreams	7
2.	Rhythm of the Ordinary	23
3.	Our California Girl	35
4.	All Good Things Come to an End	49
5.	Words That Matter	63
6.	Refusing to Settle	77
7.	Opening Pandora's Box	91
8.	Finding Our Place	105
9.	The Proper Cadence	117
10.	Ready All Along	131
11.	This is the Work	143
12.	Collectively Becoming	151
13.	The Miles Ahead	167
14.	Stepping Forward Together	177
	Epilogue	183
	Acknowledgments	189
	Appendix	191
	Endnotes	207
	About the Author	209

THE MILES WE CHASE

PROLOGUE

Every family has a story, and within that story live the lessons of love, struggle, and growth. Some stories are told at kitchen tables, passed down in voices both steady and trembling. Others live in photographs that fade with time, or in memories that surface only in the pauses between words. This book is our story, written to be remembered, shared, and lived beyond us. It's an invitation to reimagine belonging and a reminder that change begins when we refuse to accept the limits placed on what's possible. It's about the miles already traveled and the miles yet to come, the ones we chase for Ella and for every child who longs to be recognized, even when the world hasn't yet chosen to see them.

When Ella was born, nothing about the life we expected remained intact. The words spoken by doctors didn't just describe her condition, they carried the weight of assumptions about what her life would be. Before she'd taken her first steps or spoken her first words, the outlines of her future had already been limited. We were told what she might never achieve, which doors would likely remain closed, which paths weren't meant for her. Belief in what she wouldn't do seemed to arrive faster than belief in what she could, as if possibility itself had been measured, weighed, and dismissed before she even had a chance to show the world who she was.

Those judgments landed with a mix of grief and defiance. We felt the loss of the life we thought we knew, but almost in the same breath came a determination not to let others decide who our daughter could become. There were nights when fear left us hollow, yet even then a conviction began to take root, a sense that we'd have to believe in her long before the world was willing to.

And then there was Ella herself, refusing to be reduced to the words spoken about her. Even as an infant, she carried a presence that couldn't be contained by the forecasts made in hospital rooms. Her smile arrived easily, her laughter filled the air, and her spirit announced itself in ways no chart or report could predict. What others described as limitation, she turned into possibility, reminding us with every small milestone that her life would be written by joy, persistence, and the fullness of who she was, not by the boundaries others tried to draw around her.

As she developed, those boundaries followed her into classrooms. At first, school was a place of joy. She laughed with her peers, found comfort in the rhythm of routines, and carried a sense of belonging into her days. For a while, it felt like the world was opening, giving her room to grow. But beneath that promise, we began to notice how fragile it all was. Supports that once seemed steady proved uncertain. Meetings filled with paperwork and carefully measured goals often felt dimmer than the light in her eyes, much narrower than the possibility we knew she had within her. Too often, her future was spoken of in terms of limits, reduced to what she might never do instead of what she could.

And still, Ella kept showing up. She loved to learn, she loved to be among her friends, and she loved the feeling of being part of something larger than herself. Her enthusiasm didn't waver, even when opportunities fell short. Again and again she reminded us that her life wasn't going to be written by the boundaries placed around her, but by her own persistence and joy.

Watching her live with such eagerness while the system continued to narrow her path forced me to ask harder questions. Why were the structures around her so quick to measure what she lacked instead of what she brought? Why were opportunities withheld in the very places where inclusion was most needed? It became clear that love alone wouldn't be enough to shift the weight of those patterns. We'd need to understand how the system worked, where it could be moved, and how new pathways could be built. It was here, in the tension between Ella's resilience and the system's resistance, that my role as father began to merge with my role as advocate and scholar.

Now we find ourselves at a new threshold, one that asks us to dream bigger than we ever have before. For most families, a college experience is assumed possible, woven into the fabric of expectation. For us, it isn't something given. It's something we've had to imagine, prepare for, and fight to make possible. The path toward inclusive postsecondary education isn't well worn, but it's the one we've chosen, because Ella deserves nothing less than the chance to reach her full potential.

This is the work I've devoted myself to, not only as a parent but as a scholar who's studied the barriers and breakthroughs that shape opportunities for students with intellectual disabilities. Over time I've come to see that my research and Ella's journey aren't two separate accounts but one story unfolding in different dimensions. The questions I bring to my academic work are born of the life I live each day with her. And the answers I pursue aren't abstract. They're urgent, because they'll shape the future she deserves.

We're learning how to see barriers in a different way. Instead of treating them as mountains that can't be moved, we're working to understand how the system operates, where its seams are, where its weight can be shifted. We're searching for pathways that don't simply go around obstacles but create new directions altogether, routes that free us from the boundaries that have long held students like Ella back.

It would be easy to accept the system as it is. Easy to follow the outlines already drawn, to stay within the plans handed to us, to lower our expectations until they fit neatly inside the boxes schools and institutions have prepared. Easy, because ease offers rest. Ease asks little of us. Ease allows the world to move on as it always has.

But the easy path isn't the one toward big dreams. If we resign ourselves to living inside boundaries that were never meant to hold Ella's potential, then we'll never see the future she deserves. The more difficult path is the one we've chosen, the one that insists on asking different questions, building different structures, and demanding different outcomes.

When we push back against a system that's always said "this far and no further," something shifts. We start to see that the system isn't fixed. It was built, and because it was built, it can be rebuilt. And when that happens, even in small ways, it opens space for Ella and for so many others still waiting for their chance to be seen.

We're creating new pathways for Ella each day. She dreams of the kind of life every young person longs for, friendships, learning, independence, and the chance to contribute. I dream of a world that treats those desires as natural, not exceptional, and builds systems that honor them. Together, we walk with hope, fully aware of the obstacles but unwilling to let them define us.

This book is an invitation to walk with us. In these pages, you'll see our family's story, moments of triumph and heartbreak, of resilience and grace, but you'll also see the larger story of communities and educators daring to imagine something more for students like Ella. Our story isn't unusual in its love, but it's unusual in its course. It's a journey that demands persistence, faith, and the belief that the milestones we're after are worth every step.

At the end of the day, we're walking into a future that's not yet fully built, yet absolutely worth the effort. And as you turn these pages, my hope is that you'll be reminded of your own capacity to reimagine, to believe, and to create spaces where everyone belongs. Because the story of inclusive education isn't just Ella's story. It's a story that belongs to all of us, and it's found in the miles we chase together, the ones that lead us closer to a world where every dream has room to breathe.

CHAPTER 1

THE HOPES AND DREAMS

Pensacola

A messenger broke my heart one day, and in one fell swoop, while removing all semblance of spirituality, demolished everything I thought was good in this world. I've subconsciously prevented myself from ever recalling his name, remembering as little about that encounter as humanly possible.

It all started with a specialist who, over the course of two hours, brought me to a place so dark and forsaken that I simply hated him. The annoying, nonchalant nature of his voice. The diagnosis he casually outlined. Every time he said sorry and didn't mean it, because it was my pregnant wife who could barely utter a word, and our daughter whose life was already so imperfect before she was ever born. I've harbored those feelings for a long time now and if I'm being honest, I'm not keen on forgiving.

In fact, those memories have been repurposed as embers that have never died out, inspiring me to continue building the future he made sound so bleak and impossible to pursue.

And while that morning will forever be a resounding blur, I remember being at a nearby restaurant trying to order lunch, broken and undone, wondering how everything had changed so quickly. If a seemingly untroubled specialist was all we had, I didn't know if anyone would ever give a damn. And if so, whether anyone would care to help.

We had no idea what to do, who to call, or what we'd even say. So we sat there for a good while, furious at the universe, confused about what we'd done to deserve this, and unsure if tomorrow was something we'd even care for.

Six months pregnant, my wife was battling her own demons, beginning to deal with the kind of guilt only a mother would truly understand. I felt for her yet somehow managed to leave the next morning, finding myself at the corner of a conference table, my squadron commander on the other edge, awaiting words that just wouldn't come out.

The whiteboard, normally bursting on training days with color-coded diagrams and complex flight paths, was completely and eerily blank. His blue eyes were forever sharp and distinct. There was empathy in his heart. It was undeniable and I could feel it, but I still hadn't said a thing.

We sat in silence for a long while before I finally broke down, trying to explain duodenal atresia, a serious congenital heart defect, and Down syndrome. All of it crashing together as I struggled to put into words what this would mean for the baby we were expecting in just a few months.

We never ended up talking about that morning. Instead, with his unwavering support and the continued commitment from our Air Force family, I went on to move mountains that needed moving. It's taken many years to share that I broke down in that room when I was supposed to be a strong and brave officer, but the truth is, it was difficult and always will be. Perhaps I'll learn to forgive myself one day, because looking back, I'm not sure it could've happened any other way. Turns out that letting go and falling was really the first step forward.

Breakaway

Let me step out of the story for a minute.

The moment you just read about in Pensacola, the heartbreak and unraveling, is how it all began. But don't mistake this for just another emotional memoir because this book is something more. It's part reflection, part confrontation, sometimes a love letter to my family in disguise; and above all, a reckoning.

From time to time, I'll step out of the narrative and speak directly to you, like I'm doing now. These moments will feel different, and it may sound obvious, but they're meant to feel that way. Because telling the truth rarely fits into a comfortable rhythm, and if the goal is to reimagine how things could be, we'll simply have to interrupt how things have always been.

My name's Loc. I'm a husband, a father to two incredible girls, and someone who's spent years trying to make sense of this world as an outsider. As a young child I was a war refugee and after the events of September 11th, I became a commissioned officer in the US Air Force. I'm now an entrepreneur, continuing to build stories, systems, and spaces that make room for more people to thrive. I've worked with technologists in Silicon Valley, with policymakers in Sacramento, and with students of every background, from school campuses to airborne command and control platforms where knowledge was essential for survival.

This book has been a long time coming. I wasn't sure it'd come in this form, but after so many disappointing meetings, insightful conversations, and sleepless nights, it became clear the story needed to be told. Not because I have all the answers, but because families like ours are too often left alone to navigate the unknown, without the transparency and openness needed to find our way.

Although this is a uniquely personal story, it's also a universal one about social systems, the educational landscape, to an extent politics, and especially what happens when those systems decide not to make room for every kind of student. It's about how our own family has incrementally learned to fight for inclusion, how we've been carried by people we barely know, and how we've parted ways with those who were supposed to stand beside us.

At the center of it all is our daughter, Ella. And if you're intent on turning the pages and coming along for the journey, you'll get to know her. Not through the lens of what she needs or lacks, but through the fullness of who she is as a bright, joyful, and amazing teenager with endless potential.

So yes, our story starts with the broken hopes and dreams of a young family, but it surely doesn't end there. If you continue on, I'm certain our story will stay with you long after the pages are read.

Birmingham

I often remember it as a surreal, out-of-body experience. I'm seeing everything from the doorway, and it's me standing there, under the numbing buzz of fluorescent lights. Nothing registers in the background except for the bed, all the tubes, and the blinking, beeping machinery.

It was just the two of us, and for some reason, time had seemingly stood still, keeping us there for the longest moment.

Perhaps that was the space the universe needed to etch that indelible memory into our souls, that spark, the sense of purpose I'd come back to and harness when the time was right.

I was there immediately after surgery, standing at her bedside, my heart shattered into a million pieces, devastated by what she'd already endured. It was Ella and she was barely two days old, not yet given the chance to indulge in her mother's embrace, so quickly separated and sent with others before even the first hello.

We were worlds apart from anything considered home, and I felt helpless, overwhelmed by the piercing, burning guilt. I knew then I'd suffer an eternity for her to experience a world without torment, but I also knew those hopes were in vain. Because regardless of the burden I chose to bear, this was to be her introduction to this world, and my first foray into fatherhood.

Three days passed, and we all pushed forth. Like the miracle she's always been, Ella fought against the torment with such grace and strength. Despite everything she was already up against, I remember her looking so peaceful and content. She recovered quickly, free from all the tubing, breathing on her own, and sometimes even choosing to scream out loud, letting the world know she'd arrived. We were finally able to hold her for a few minutes, kiss her, and tell her that we'd always be there by her side.

The space inside of Birmingham Children's Hospital became our own kind of world in those moments, one that neither slept nor stopped. Day and night bled into one another, creating a cycle of constant monitoring, feeding attempts, and updates from the nurses we came to know. The outside world faded, and all that mattered was what happened inside those walls.

Another five weeks passed under the care of the most compassionate pediatric nurses, recovering, growing, and learning to take the smallest amounts of milk. We were finally blessed enough to leave the hospital and take her home. And though we weren't exactly ready to care for someone so dependent on us for her livelihood, we managed to figure things out, if only one small step at a time. Awake for the better part of each and every night, we devoted ourselves to keeping her healthy and preparing her for the challenges to come.

Leaving Birmingham Children's marked a turning point for all of us, a monumental step toward life in the real world. By then, our makeshift existence in Alabama had taken on a unique kind of charm, becoming an endearing part of our journey. I still remember the look on our nurse's face, anxious and full of hesitation, as we gently buckled Ella into the 4Runner. Her tiny body disappeared into the infant car seat, facing backwards and nestled safely in the rear.

As would always be the case, her mom sat beside her, while I cruised down the Alabama freeway, barely reaching forty-five miles an hour, cautious of every single bump in the road. I imagine it wasn't easy watching us drive away, allowing this fragile little girl into the world.

Life outside the hospital walls came quickly, and we did our best to shape it into something steady. During one of our earliest road trips from Panama City, we'd found a small two-bedroom apartment tucked into a suburban corner of Birmingham with just enough space for us, and the steady stream of friends and family who traveled from afar to offer their support. You may have heard of Hoover before, a high school football town made famous by MTV in the early 2000s as reality television was beginning to take shape.

It wasn't my first time in Alabama though. Years earlier, I'd completed Officer School in Montgomery, back when my understanding of duty was still shaped by protocol and tradition, not yet tested by fatherhood. Never in a million years had I expected to return under circumstances like these. And yet, there we were, living a life anchored by events so unexpected.

It'd be strange to say without context, but Birmingham is never far from my thoughts. The whimsical nature of it all still lingers affectionately in the background. It has, and will forever, define our life together, as the most remarkable, most adventurous, most emotional journey ever.

Breakaway

If it all feels like a lot, that's because it was. Our time at Birmingham Children's Hospital continues to shape everything that followed. It's hard to pinpoint a single moment, but in that season, something meaningful began to take root. It was a quiet awakening that revealed new strength, deeper awareness, and a clearer sense of what truly matters.

Inside that hospital room, surrounded by the harsh lights and steady monitors, I became a father in the truest sense. Through every passing hour and every act of care, I learned what it meant to be fully present. I began to see life not in terms of accomplishments or timelines, but in connection to something greater, and in the simple power of love that asks for nothing in return.

We didn't plan for it or see it coming, but Birmingham offered a kind of clarity we'd never known. It redefined our sense of home and expanded our understanding of family. It gave us purpose and helped us begin to shape the life we wanted to build together, with care and with intention.

As this book unfolds, I invite you to feel, to reimagine, and to believe in a world that welcomes every kind of learner and every kind of dream. Through these moments of reflection, I hope we can shape something meaningful together, a shared understanding, a greater compassion, and a deeper commitment to a better tomorrow.

Las Vegas

Finally in Vegas, beyond the shadows of decadence and wildly lavish dreams, there was light, and a sense that perhaps someone was watching from above. It wasn't where we'd imagined ourselves to be, yet amidst a desert borne of self-indulgence and greed, we were given the chance to mend a failing heart.

By the time we'd landed on that chilly December afternoon, Ella was barely four months old, a tiny thing who'd overcome so much in life, but was incessantly asked to endure. Her feedings were struggles lasting hours on end, mostly futile attempts at the smallest amounts of milk and syringe-fed medications that made a daunting process even worse. It sounds so ordinary, a baby taking her milk, yet it consumed and frustrated us, through the days and nights that seemed to never end.

Somehow though, she had to grow, and bear those months of suffocating pressure to gain the weight and the strength she so desperately needed. It was disheartening to say the least, and almost impossible to accept, but our goal in raising Ella was to allow her an open heart surgery, to save her life. And no matter how hard we tried to wish it away, we always knew that as soon as we could, we'd take the chance to make things right. So we fled across the States, bringing everything we had, the hopes and dreams that seemed lost those months ago.

It was a huge rush as we settled into yet another temporary life. A new set of military orders had purposefully brought us west, and all that mattered was the calendar at this point and the days leading to her surgery. Between getting acclimated on base and figuring out where we were going to eventually live, we tried our best to make it through the uncertainty, living out of those large suitcases that held everything we needed. Everything felt so fragile at that point. Every ounce of milk, every breath, every tiny movement.

The day came in early December and I'll never forget how she stared back at me from the nurse's arms, not knowing where she was. I kissed her one last time and handed her over. Her innocence, those fluorescent lights again, a tiny hospital gown, and dark questioning eyes, wondering why. It was the first time I'd ever left her side, forcing myself to turn and walk away, knowing I'd moved every single mountain I could. She was under someone else's watch now, and somehow or another our lives would change.

That afternoon in the hospital, when we finally heard she'd made it through, I exhaled for the first time since Pensacola, and all the emotions of our incredible journey came rushing out. I don't remember ever crying so hard.

Unfortunately, the recovery seemed to be as grueling as the procedure itself. If you've ever seen someone after an open-heart procedure, it's difficult to imagine the trauma their body's been through. She cried often in pain, and our own hearts continued to break as we stayed with her in that hospital room through eight days of recovery, never seeing much of the outside world.

There were long hours of silence, where all we could do was sit beside her, hold her hand, and whisper that she was brave, that she was strong, and that she was loved. We rarely slept. And in those moments, when her heart found its rhythm again, there was an appreciation for the present moment that made everything else seem irrelevant.

We didn't take turns so much as we folded ourselves into a narrow pull-out chair, trying to catch a few hours of rest before the next movement. The room was never still as the monitors chirped in steady rhythm, and nurses came in throughout the night, soft-spoken, focused, always careful. Sleep was shallow, and yet it felt like enough. Because through it all, we were with her. And in that closeness, even in the fatigue, there was lasting gratitude for her breath, for the healing underway, and for the kindness that surrounded us.

Day by day, she revealed strength in its purest form. Her breaths grew deeper, her color returned with warmth, her cries rose with a new clarity that filled the room. What once felt fragile began to steady, as if she was finally finding herself. Every small change carried its own message, a reminder that she was growing, reaching, and becoming more of who she was meant to be.

It was nothing short of a miracle.

She eventually started becoming an entirely different baby and was taking her milk like never before. With a fully functioning heart for the first time, she was ready to grow and find her place in this world. I'll be forever grateful and indebted to the wonderful people who brought light into our world, who helped mend a failing heart, who gave a beautiful baby her first, full breath of life. Theirs are truly the hands that heal.

Little did I know that what we started with Ella all those years ago was really the prelude to an ongoing pursuit of happiness, a story we'd go on to tell, with intertwining chapters for years to come. We brought Ella home a few days before Christmas, and life started. Again.

Breakaway

Yes, this is Ella's story, but it's also ours.

If you've made it this far, if you're still reading, I just want to say thank you. Instead of contemplating a polished novel or something more refined, I've spent many years slowly recalling how it all felt in real life. It's a story about figuring things out as you go and holding onto what matters most.

You know, during the first part of this journey with Ella, something in me began to shift. I began thinking deeply about what I wanted to stand for as a father, what kind of legacy I might leave, and how our family could build a future that honored not just responsibility but also gratefulness and joy.

I noticed the way Ella grew with our love. I watched my wife give everything she had to care for our daughter, and I felt the power of kindness when strangers offered support in their own, unique ways. Those moments have all stayed with me, and they constantly remind me that a meaningful life is not something handed to you. Rather, it's something you shape through time and with intention. It grows through care and presence, and through the choices you make every day to show up for the people who matter most.

If there's one truth I brought forth from those early days, it's that every moment mattered. Pensacola's heartbreak pushed us into the depths of grief, but it also gave us the fire to rise again. Birmingham's endless nights tested us, but they also showed us how grace can be found in the smallest acts of care. Las Vegas brought fear to its sharpest point, but it also delivered the gift of healing, a heart renewed, and a baby ready to grow.

Together, those places became more than chapters in our story. They became proof that even in the hardest seasons, something beautiful can take root. Ella showed us that miracles don't arrive fully formed. They grow day by day, in deeper breaths, in brighter color, and in cries that personify new strength.

These were the first miles we traveled, and they'll always mark the beginning of the path ahead. From the very start, Ella's taught us that hope is resilient, that it refuses to fade as it continues moving us forward.

CHAPTER 2

RHYTHM OF THE ORDINARY

After nearly two weeks at Sunrise Children's Hospital, we were finally home, admiring the beautiful Christmas tree standing in the corner of our living room. And for a little while things actually felt steady again. It wasn't perfect, and it wasn't without effort, but it became comfortable in a way that allowed us to take deep, full breaths. We fell into a routine that carried us from one day to the next, and there was joy in the rhythm of ordinary life. Bottles, medications, diaper changes, and follow-up visits. It all became part of who we were.

In the evenings, after Ella would go to bed, my wife and I would sit together on the couch and catch a few episodes of Dexter while the dinner plates soaked in the sink. We would laugh and cringe at the dark humor, and for the first time in a long while, it felt like contentment would be something we'd soon feel again. It reminded us we were okay, and somehow, still whole.

Ella took to her bottles with the kind of ease we hadn't seen before. What once felt like a fragile negotiation now became something natural and joyful. She drank with hunger and purpose, and with each feeding, her cheeks rounded out, and her arms grew soft with Michelin baby rolls. Our tall kitchen counter was repurposed, holding rows of bottles and baby essentials, all laid out with care and thoughtfulness.

In many ways, this routine became a quiet form of devotion to raising our daughter, and over time, the repetition brought a sense of calm I still think about to this day. It's difficult finding the perfect words, but it felt like the bubble from the Truman show had enveloped our family, creating a protective space within which to cherish this new lease on life.

On the weekdays, I'd drop by Trader Joe's to pick up groceries and maybe some flowers for the kitchen table, and though it may sound mundane, these small errands grounded us in real life. Most nights when I was home, I'd make dinner and we'd sit down for a meal with the Kardashians living out their outrageous lives on television. I suppose we were learning how to live again by simply being in the moment.

We were grateful for the new home that held us and allowed our family to heal.

By no means though, had life become the perfect fairy tale. In fact, the monitors still remained by her crib, quietly humming through the night. The small, transportable oxygen tanks were still being delivered to our door each week. And that feeling of subtle, yet constant alertness ambled in the background like a soft drumbeat. We never mentioned it much, but we felt it all the same.

Then came the morning when I was getting ready for base, stepping into my flight suit and gathering my things. Ella was in the living room, calmly taking her bottle. Her mother asked me to come over with a steady and focused voice, the kind that signals something's worth paying attention to. I knelt beside her, and for a while I watched, but could barely tell that Ella's breathing seemed a little off. There was a subtle strain in how she drew each breath, but otherwise everything looked fine.

Later that afternoon, guided by a mother's intuition and the kind of knowing that comes only from experience, they drove to Nellis AFB to see her pediatrician. I can't remember her name now, but I remember how she always made us feel heard and cared for. Within hours of her thorough examination and some deliberation over whether to send them home, I received a call at my desk and we were in an ambulance, heading once again to Sunrise Children's.

It turned out to be pulmonary hypertension, a rare but serious complication that can emerge after heart surgery. It's the kind of diagnosis that often goes unnoticed until it becomes something far more serious. But this time, we caught it early because her mother was there to notice the nuances that only someone so attuned to her would ever feel.

That quiet chain of events, all unrushed and purposeful, may have changed everything.

We were back in the hospital world we thought we'd finally left behind, all the monitors and sensors, and the cool stillness of those rooms. I stood beside her crib yet again, watching her chest rise and fall beneath the weight of all those wires, thinking about how familiar it all felt.

After a few days of extensive testing and steady observation, including a follow-up from her heart surgeon, we were cleared to bring her home once more. This time, she came with a prescription for compounded Sildenafil and another set of those tiny syringes.

We had a fresh calendar of cardiology appointments lined up at the clinic just around the way, and that same pulse oximeter still sat beside our bed, attached to her toe, blinking methodically through the night.

As expected, sleep was hard to come by as our minds worked to catch up with reality once again. We checked her oxygen levels more often than we needed to, replayed the surgeon's words in our heads, and watched each breath she took.

Breakaway

Before we move on, I just wanted to sit with this for a second. Because the truth is you never really know what's coming in this life. One day you're laughing at something on the couch, and then suddenly, you're back under hospital lights, staring at monitors again, trying to remember how to breathe.

That's how life works sometimes, without warning and certainly without asking. And no matter how experienced you think you are, it still finds a way to shake you. I've learned though, that just because life is unpredictable doesn't mean you have to live in fear of it. In fact, that kind of fear steals from you. It robs you of the good while it's happening. And if you're not careful, you'll miss the very moments that were meant to carry you through.

Henderson

Something about Las Vegas worked for us. The desert heat could be relentless, but the community of Henderson welcomed us in ways we never expected.

Most people only know the Vegas that's in the movies, the casinos, the glamour and neon nights. But just beyond all that, in the quieter neighborhoods and master planned communities are families just like ours. Just regular folks working to provide for their families and hustling from one day to the next.

That fall, we hosted Thanksgiving in the city we never expected to live in, inside an apartment we never thought would feel like home. My parents came, along with my brother and a few family members. Some local friends were also there, including a couple raising their own daughter with Down syndrome. I was still very much an amateur cook back then, but I still managed to set up an offset smoker in the driveway and spent hours tending to a turkey. I ended up having to finish the cook in the oven, just to have it ready for dinner, but the experience was nevertheless a memorable one.

Amazingly enough, our little apartment made room for every single person. People sat wherever they could, on the arms of couches, on folding chairs we pulled from the garage, even on pillows we brought out from the bedrooms. The counters were packed with everything from green bean casseroles to mashed potatoes to stuffing with sausage and sage. It wasn't anything fancy, but at the same time, it all felt so familiar.

When it finally came time to carve the turkey, I just picked up a carving knife and started. No one said anything, but everyone gathered around to marvel at the sight. Quite honestly, this is what we'd pictured when we first talked about starting a family. Not a flawless holiday painting come to life, but something real that you could wrap your arms around, very much like having smoked turkey for the first time during Thanksgiving and passing around extra mashed potatoes made with tons of butter. You know, like how family feels in the best possible way.

Of course, Ella was there through all of it, hanging out in the living room as she always does, wide-eyed and glowing. She was soaking it all in, all the smiling faces, the sound of familiar laughter, and the warmth of people who loved her. She was the center of it, and maybe for the first time, we let ourselves believe that this moment, this messy, beautiful holiday in the desert, was always meant to be ours.

In the quiet months that followed, Ella's therapy became part of our home. She would cruise along the couch with growing confidence, one hand pressed into the cushions, the other reaching out toward her iPad, which rested like a small beacon just within reach. It played her favorite Signing Time! videos on loop, songs she already knew by heart, even if she couldn't sing them yet. And without anyone coaxing her, she began to stand taller, learned how to sign a few words, and started becoming the Ella we know today.

Some weekends, we'd give her mom to relax, so Ella and I would drive off to continue building our own little tradition. I'd take her to Einstein's bagel shop just around the corner on Eastern Avenue. It wasn't anything special, just the warmth of the morning sun through the windows, the faint scent of fresh bagels in the air, and coffee that was always strong enough to help you feel awake.

I'd go through the same routine each time. Grab the heavy wooden high chair. Wipe down the table. Set her cushion just right. Place the bottle in front of her. And then I'd finally sit down. She would watch it all, like a little conductor keeping track of every move. And when I was done, she'd look up and offer me the sweetest smile. As if to say, now we can begin.

There was something so endearing about those mornings. The low hum of conversations we weren't a part of. The way the desert sun would seep through the store front and make the place so comfortable and inviting. It was all so ordinary, but I remember it so fondly. A space where we didn't need anything more than what we had.

Sometimes I'd look at her there, and I'd drift back to that morning before she was born. It hadn't been that long, considering she was just a year old, but it felt like we'd lived many lifetimes in between. I remember stepping outside our Hoover apartment with no intention of really going anywhere, but just to be somewhere else for a while. The southern air was already warming up, thick with the kind of humidity you knew would only get heavier. I stayed close, circling the edge of the lot, feeling the early sun on my skin. I wasn't trying to figure anything out. I just had to let all the questions settle a little. What if I can't do this? What if she needs more than I know how to give? And when I felt ready, I went back inside and life went on.

In the evenings, after Ella had gone to bed, I would sometimes hear the gentle rhythm of my wife moving through the kitchen. The soft brush cleansing bottles from the day, and water running steadily against the bottom of the sink. We didn't always speak. Sometimes we just passed each other in the hallway, slowly and quietly, offering nothing more than a glance or a brief touch on the shoulder. But every now and then, we would sit on the edge of the couch with no distractions at all, just the two of us breathing the same air.

I saw her resilience and strength, and admired how much she'd brought to this journey of ours. She could read Ella's needs without saying a word. She could carry exhaustion with the grace of someone who had decided long ago that quitting wasn't an option. She could carve out space for joy even when it felt so far away. I'd watched her make Ella's meals, care for all of her many essentials, and support her in every sense of the word, and I came to believe something I hadn't before. That none of this was random. And that we were surely meant to be Ella's parents, even if so many of those reasons hadn't been revealed to us quite yet.

During those days, my hours stretched between two worlds. One built on orders and salutes, the other on softness and presence. On Nellis Air Force Base, the rhythm was predictable. Protocols, ranks, routines. You moved with in tention, you spoke with clarity, and there was no room for hesitation or vulnerability. But when I came home and hung up the uniform, all of that loosened. Ella needed something different and softer. There were no scripts here. Neither flowcharts nor briefings on how to do right by your family. Just the instincts and presence of someone learning to be a father despite how difficult it seemed to be.

Somehow, perhaps coaxed by Ella's grace, all of it began to weave together. The therapy sessions. The scent of slow burning coals curling through the driveway that Thanksgiving. The stillness of bagel shop mornings. The soft sound of running water in the kitchen. It all became part of our rhythm, one that was intended to help us stay grounded, to return again and again.

All the while, the world around us kept turning as it always does. Some of our friends packed up and left. Orders shifted and short deployments came and went. But we stayed in that small corner of Henderson, in a desert city known more for distraction than for peace, and in that space, we built a life that asked nothing more of us than to be fully present. We didn't need bright lights or loud declarations. We had routines we could count on, the kindness of our community, and a rhythm we could trust.

Breakaway

I just want to close this chapter by telling you this.

Sometimes the start of something good doesn't feel good at all. It feels like doubt. It feels like fear. It feels like trying to smile while holding your breath, like doing your best not to fall apart in a parking lot or a hospital lobby or your own living room.

And I guess what I've learned is that you don't need to feel strong to be strong. You just need to keep going. You just need to stay present. Because there's something remarkably admirable in showing up for a life you don't fully understand yet. And one day, you'll look back and realize this was the moment the story really began.

So if you're ready, I'll keep going. Because there's more to tell. And you deserve to hear it all.

Henderson may not have been the place we imagined for ourselves, but it became the place we needed. It gave us mornings filled with sunlight, evenings wrapped in quiet rituals, and a community that reminded us we weren't alone. Most of all, it gave Ella space to grow into herself, to take her first steps toward becoming the joyful person we know today.

In that season, life taught us gently. We learned that strength can rise from the simplest routines, that love can steady itself in the ordinary, and that belonging often begins right where you are. What felt like small moments at the time were always laying the foundation for everything to come.

It was never just a stop along the way. That desert city became the ground beneath the first steps of a greater journey, the place where our family discovered not only how to survive, but how to live again.

Viva Las Vegas.

CHAPTER 3
OUR CALIFORNIA GIRL

Nellis Air Force Base, about thirty-five minutes northeast of Henderson, offered our military family something rare in the form of much needed stability. While I was maintaining a productive and incredibly consistent schedule on base, my wife cared for her at home, managing a recurring series of therapies and appointments, keeping her healthy and engaged, and pushing for every inch of incremental progress. Despite not having family close by or any built-in support system, we created environments that allowed Ella to recover and thrive. The Henderson community showed up for us in ways we never would've imagined, our Air Force family gave unconditionally, and the medical community, highly skilled and competent, became a source of strength we came to rely on.

As we began giving more of ourselves to Henderson, the city responded in kind and allowed us to focus on strengthening our foundation. It also gave Ella the chance to stretch out and explore. There were still challenges, of course, but there was also an inclusive world developing around us. From therapists and doctors to friends and neighbors, from military colleagues to strangers in the community, it felt like this part of Vegas, against every assumption we had, was becoming the perfect place to raise a family.

Looking back, we probably would've benefited from staying a bit longer, but in reality, it was always meant to be a short stay. Just as we were all settling in, our time in Henderson's serene Seven Hills neighborhood came to an end. I'd extended my Air Force commitment by two years when I accepted the assignment at Nellis, and now that contract was coming to an end. After eight and a half years of service, including a European tour with NATO, it was finally time to step away. For many reasons, we were excited though, ready to transition back to civilian life and make our way to California, closer to family and friends, closer to what we envisioned would be a more stable and connected future.

The final weeks were quieter than I expected. There were a few outbound tasks, a handful of farewell handshakes, and as expected, kind words about how I'd be missed, how I'd left the place better than I found it. Whether that was true or not, I suppose I'll never know. What I do remember is standing in the back of the squadron room after my last Commander's call, still in uniform, unsure whether to linger or just walk out. One of our civilian contractors, a career Air Force veteran himself, tapped me on the shoulder and thanked me for my service. I nodded and said very little. Not because I was ungrateful, but because I didn't yet have the words. That huge chapter was ending, and I hadn't made sense of it all just yet.

The last time I put on my flight suit, I told myself to remember this, to take it in slowly, because I'd never feel it again. I tried to breathe deep enough to hold the moment in place, as if memory could be etched into muscle and fabric. It wasn't just a uniform, it was years of discipline, identity, and the weight of service stitched into every seam.

When the moment passed, I returned to the quiet of our Henderson apartment, surrounded by boxes and the shuffle of movers. What surprised me most was the silence that lingered, especially in the evenings when everything grew still. Ella and her mom had already gone ahead to California, I was leaving the squadron, and for the first time in years, it was just me.

There was no ceremony at the squadron or anything special since we come and go so often in the military. And it wasn't like I was retiring from decades of service or anything, so there wasn't a folded flag or parting salute, just a deep-seated recognition of a remarkable experience that lasted for over eight years. I had given everything I could to this country. In return, I was offered a home when I was a younger man and uncertain about the world, especially after the events of 9/11. That home gave me the utmost sense of purpose and lifelong friends who feel exactly the same way about our time together. And when Ella came into the world, fragile and fighting from the start, it gave me the security and the freedom to care for her in all the ways she needed. Ultimately, the Air Force helped me become the father I was destined to be, and I tell folks all the time that I'd walk the same path all over again in a heartbeat.

I still have every part of my uniform. The wings that took so long to earn, a collection of velcro name tags from all the different squadrons I'd joined, and all the decorations and patches I'd accumulated over the years. Everything's securely stored away, tucked into a few storage bins, sitting on one of our shelves. I'm okay with knowing I won't ever wear any of those uniforms again, but the fact that they're there, and that I'd worn them during my time of service, means more than I can ever express. One of these days I might have some grandkids and I'll tell them about the life and times of Captain Nguyen in our United States Air Force.

When it came time, we left Las Vegas with hope in our hearts. Her mom and I were preparing to dive into the corporate world and to continue growing our young family. The ground was feeling slightly more solid beneath our feet, and we told ourselves that California, a progressive and well-resourced state, would be the best place in the country for a little girl with Down syndrome.

Breakaway

Henderson showed us something we hadn't really understood before. Belonging isn't something handed down by a system or guaranteed just because you stay in a place long enough. It happens when people choose to see you and walk with you. For us, it wasn't family nearby or a built-in network that carried us. It was therapists who believed Ella's progress mattered, neighbors who showed up without hesitation, and colleagues who treated our challenges like they were their own.

That kind of community can't be measured in years or geography because it changes how you think about home. We started to realize that inclusion isn't about squeezing into a space that's already built, but about shaping it together so there's room for everyone. And once you've lived that kind of belonging, you carry it with you. It stays as an expectation, a responsibility, and as proof of what's possible.

The next few years of Ella's life remained full of appointments, but they carried a sense of purpose, almost a rhythm we could depend on. She was quickly enrolled in early intervention services through the county, and several times a week, we made our way to therapy centers throughout the valley. It became part of our routine, and the offices and waiting rooms became easier to recognize. There were physical therapists with brightly colored mats who would gently stretch and position her limbs while coaxing her through with songs and toys. There was a speech therapist who became our mentor, never rushed, always attentive, shaping sounds into syllables and syllables into words. And the occupational therapist who celebrated every new grasp of a crayon or utensil, reminding us that it was her job to develop those fine motor skills, and our job as parents to simply love our daughter.

Some days, Ella just wouldn't be in the mood and refused to cooperate with any of her therapists. Other days, she would be energized, eager to participate and learn all these new skills. And while there were always setbacks, and intense moments of frustration and doubt, there was a sense that something good was unfolding.

And then, right in the middle of it all, something happened that changed everything. We found out we were expecting another baby. Ella was going to be a big sister. It was a girl. Another daughter. And for reasons I still can't fully explain, that news felt sacred. It was as if life itself was reminding us that even in the middle of uncertainty, beauty has a way of breaking through. She would be born here in California, in the place we had chosen with hope in our hearts, and somehow her arrival made that choice feel even more right.

Even before she was born, her presence began shaping our days. We talked about her incessantly. We made room for her both literally and figuratively while imagining all the ways she and Ella would grow up together. It was no longer just about surviving or staying on track. It was about creating something lasting, a future for both of our girls. And in that incredible shift, something softened. The stress didn't go away. The hard moments didn't vanish. But joy started taking up space again. And it reminded us why we were doing all of this in the first place.

When Cady was born, life took us in an entirely new direction. Not only did she add to the family dynamic, but she transformed us exponentially in ways only she was capable of. She was the sweetest, most gentle newborn we could've ever hoped for. So calm and so easy to love. Caring for her felt instinctive, natural, even in the blur of exhaustion. It was as if she had arrived already knowing her place in our little family, content to fill it with grace.

Raising Cady felt almost surreal in its simplicity. She was strong and vocal from the start, alert and self-aware, almost as if she arrived into the world already comfortable in her skin. Her needs were clear, her rhythms were steady, and the only real challenge was that she refused to take a bottle when her mom was away, which made feeding her a little stressful at times. But even then, it felt manageable, even normal. And maybe that was the difference this time around. After everything we had navigated with Ella, raising Cady reminded us what ease could feel like. For the most part, we watched her meet milestones ahead of schedule as she taught herself how to become a toddler, each miraculous step reminding us we weren't always fighting uphill. The fact that she complemented her sister in such instinctive ways was another sign that none of this was happening by chance.

Ella was three when she met her sister. We still laugh when we remember those first few days. Without being asked or guided, she began tossing stuffed animals and blankets into Cady's crib. Not forcefully or in protest, but as if she understood on a deeper level that this was another little one, someone small like her who needed things, too. Her version of welcoming her sister was so practical and endearing, and entirely perfect.

But those early weeks weren't as easy as we tend to remember. We had moved into a somewhat spacious two-bedroom apartment at that point. Although Ella now had her own room, she was still waking up several times each night. She consistently wandered out around two or three in the morning, and we'd have to be ready to guide her back to bed, soothe her, and try again. And then, as all newborns do, Cady would naturally stir for her next feeding and diaper change. Mom would feed the newborn while I stayed up with Ella, and together we moved through those nights, dividing and conquering, and surviving what became the most exhausting time of our lives.

At a certain point, I moved into the living room and slept on the couch for months. It was just too difficult with Ella waking in the middle of the night, and we were so conscious of her wandering into Cady's space, disrupting those precious stretches when she was finally sleeping soundly. So we adapted in ways that probably looked strange from the outside, staging ourselves like a night crew on rotation. Eventually, we moved our entire mattress set into the living room so Cady could have her own quiet room as well. Sure, it was unconventional. But it worked. And for that, I was grateful.

Still, even with such a beautiful family around me, something heavier had started to settle in. A quiet sense of doubt and a feeling that I was drifting away from who I used to be. Sure, I had stepped out of the uniform, but I hadn't fully stepped into whatever came next. The work I was doing didn't feel like mine. The days were incredibly busy, but at the same time, I felt so completely empty. And the hardest part was that it all looked fine on the surface. I'd started a new career, we had two healthy girls and a roof over our heads. But deep inside, I felt like I was losing a part of myself I didn't know how to get back. There was always a dark cloud overhead, suffocating at times, keeping me from enjoying what should've been some of Cady's earliest, brightest days. I know I didn't use the word back then, but if I'm being honest, it was depression. And I should have asked for help.

Fortunately, somewhere in that shadow, I started to find a way forward, out of necessity and for the sake of my daughters and an incredible wife who'd already walked through so much with me. I knew that if anything was going to change, it had to start with me. So I leaned on myself harder than I ever had before. I worked longer. I asked more questions. I started connecting with anyone who would listen, and made it my mission to find something better. Something that felt more like me.

Eventually, I found work that challenged me and a career I could align with for the time being. I asked for new responsibilities, sought out different roles across the organization, and when the opportunities came, I showed up ready every single time. Because I knew what was at stake, and I wasn't going to let my family down.

There was even a stretch of time when I used to arrive at the office around six in the morning, long before any meetings began. With the first of maybe four coffees in hand, I would read and study, pouring over materials I barely understood at first. By the time my colleagues arrived, I already had three hours of quiet preparation under my belt. I did that every day, week after week, until I became knowledgeable in my own right. And then something shifted. Slowly, the learning turned into competence. The unfamiliar language of software development and web application security started to make sense. I began to thrive in the role I had carved out for myself, earned the respect of my colleagues and our clients, and started regaining what I'd lost when I'd hung up that uniform, the momentum to keep moving forward.

It's why, even now, I'm continuing to help others make that transition from active duty into civilian life, providing more guidance and allowing for more grace. My hope is that other veterans don't have to go through what I did. I didn't know how hard it would be to give up the uniform. I didn't know how much of myself I had left behind. And I didn't know how many pieces I'd need to rebuild before I felt whole again.

Breakaway

Veterans don't always name it. We move forward. We manage. We carry the weight alone and convince ourselves that hard nights are just part of the transition, that losing our identity is a temporary cost, and that whatever we're feeling will pass if we just keep going. But what I've come to understand, what I wish I'd recognized back then, is that depression doesn't always arrive with thunder. Sometimes it's overlooked as you're going through the motions. You're just watching the world smile around you and wondering why you can't feel the same way.

And when no one talks about it, we start to think that silence is strength.

But strength can mean something else entirely. It can mean picking up the phone. Walking into a clinic. Saying the thing you've avoided for months. It can mean asking for help not because you're broken, but because you're ready to feel whole again. It can mean looking at the people you love most and realizing they've always seen the best in you, even when you couldn't.

If you're having a difficult time and something feels off, even if you can't explain it, I hope you won't wait. I hope you won't let it grow in the hidden corners of your life. Talk to someone. Say something out loud. Because there's no courage in suffering silently. The courage is in choosing to come back to yourself.

We believed, back then, that if we kept the pace and trusted the process, the system would guide Ella the way it was meant to. California felt like promise itself, with its well-funded districts, its respected hospitals, and its progressive reputation. It seemed to point toward a future where she would be lifted, not limited. We were still learning, but belief has a way of moving you forward even when the path ahead is unclear.

In the quiet spaces of our days, though, questions began to surface. What would happen when the supports faded, when the system asked her to mold herself to its shape instead of reshaping to hers? How long would the rhythm hold before the song changed? We didn't recognize it then, but the gentle cocoon of early intervention was already thinning, preparing to give way to the sharper edges of school systems and expectations never written with Ella in mind.

For the time being, though, we had a Southern belle from Birmingham and a California girl to care for, and they filled our world with light. Each routine, each appointment, each small triumph became a kind of devotion, a steady weaving of something that felt lasting. It was the beginning of so much more. And in that season, with both girls at the heart of our days, life stretched open like morning sky, wide enough to hold our fears and still leave room for hope.

Even now, when I look back, I know those years were not just about finding balance. They were about learning how to believe, how to stay present, and how to trust that love, in all its ordinary forms, could prepare us for everything still to come.

CHAPTER 4
ALL GOOD THINGS COME TO AN END

We made it through the hardest stretch. Or at least, that's what we believed. Our days had settled into something steady, and our girls were happy and growing. There was good energy in the house, and even through the blur of exhaustion, there was laughter. Sure, we realized that simply being in California wasn't going to fix everything, but we now had a supporting cast of family and friends nearby. And for a time, that felt like enough.

But just because life steadies out for a moment doesn't mean the coast is clear, and that became increasingly obvious as Ella grew out of her toddler days and inched closer to preschool. It started gradually with a few flickers of hesitation and developed into a persistent truth we couldn't ignore, a dismal feeling suggesting that the road ahead was about to narrow. Conversations with specialists felt more uncertain. The warmth and structure that defined her early care began to give way to new terminology and systems, and we were being asked to trust a process we didn't yet understand.

We were, in fact, preparing to step into the world of public education, into the realm of assessments and eligibility, acronyms and paperwork. With every meeting and every form, it became harder to deny what was taking shape. Unlike what our naive minds had imagined, the public education system wasn't preparing to welcome Ella with intention and support. Instead, it was preparing to categorize her, and measure her against the stereotypical idea of what a student with Down syndrome is capable of achieving. Ultimately, without ever saying it out loud, the system was already dictating how far she'd go in this world.

It's one thing to move mountains in a hospital room, when the crisis is clear and the stakes are obvious. But what happens when those mountains are entire institutions unto themselves, ones that were built upon outdated beliefs? What happens when the challenge is not surviving to see another day, but rather belonging to society everyday? When the urgency is lost, and the resistance comes disguised as an endless cycle of processes and procedures?

We were about to find out because the next hill to climb would require more than just our energy and optimism. In fact, it would require something much deeper and grounded. Like the unwavering belief that our daughter's worth would never be compromised, a refusal to let her future be defined by checklists and protocols, and most importantly, a deep commitment to moving forward, even when the path was unclear.

That was the next chapter in our journey, rooted in the space between what inclusion theoretically looks like and how it's actually personified in real life.

As Ella approached pre-K, and as we started imagining what her first school experiences might be like, what little momentum we'd gained since Vegas began to stall. The things that once guided us like medical plans, structured therapies, and clearly defined milestones, began to fade into uncertainty. And as the conversations shifted from personal development to categorical placement, from available services to potential eligibility, we realized we were entering a new landscape, one filled with complicated rules we didn't yet understand.

We'd spent years moving forward and piecing together a world where Ella would grow. But now, that world was being shaped by institutions we had no real relationship with, and systems that seemed far more interested in what she could not do than in who she was becoming. There was no orientation to this world either. Just an understanding that everything was about to get more complicated. And for the first time we were no longer driving the process. We were being pulled into something shaped by people who had long ago formed their own ideas about a child like ours.

It became painfully clear that the world around Ella would need to evolve in order to support her continued growth. The problem was, we had no idea how that would happen. And worse, we had this growing sense that the people in charge of that world had little understanding of who she was in the first place. Not to mention the person she was destined to become.

As a newborn, her medical care had been exceptional, and early intervention came with structure and clarity. There were specialists, development plans, and tangible goals. But as we began thinking about what inclusion might really look like, and what it would mean for her to be part of a classroom community, things became much more vague. I remember attending a meeting about IEPs and special education placements, walking out confused and unsettled. I couldn't quite name it then, but the feeling was so visceral. Instead of being welcomed to a system that would support us moving forward, we were being prepared for arguments, debates, and legal battles against that very system, all of which sounded like nothing we'd imagined.

It was a difficult realization and one we never expected to face. The idea that families and schools could find themselves on opposite sides of the table felt disorienting. And as a result, we became somewhat cautious and wary of the steps ahead.

Our early meetings with the district only added to the doubt. Everything was driven by procedures, timelines, checklists, and required signatures. It felt like each person brought a file to review, data to present, and a script to follow.

There was one IEP meeting that stayed with me for years. We came in ready to talk about Ella's growth, what her days looked like, and how she was developing academically. But instead, we spent nearly the entire session reviewing page after page of assessment data. Sure, the statistics all proved that she was drastically below grade level in every area. But sadly enough, none of that data was remotely helpful. We were wasting precious time together pouring through percentiles when we could've been discussing real-life teaching strategies and exploring relevant approaches to skills development. There must have been six or seven of us in the room, so you do the math and figure out how much that unproductive session cost the system.

To be clear, it wasn't that the teachers and specialists in the room didn't care. Some of them clearly did. In fact, I believe many of them chose this work for the most sincere and selfless reasons. Special education is not something you fall into. It's a calling. A commitment to supporting students who deserve the most care. But even the most dedicated educators can be worn down over time by the pressure, the paperwork, and the constant grind of compliance. Slowly, the system begins to reshape them. It narrows their work to timelines and technicalities, stifles their capacity to connect, and pulls them further from the reason they started in the first place. And before long, they're no longer doing the work they set out to do.

This is the part no one really wants to say out loud, at least not in public. Because it's both ironic and incredibly disappointing to realize that the very system built to support our most vulnerable students is also the one that can slowly harden the people who care about them most. To be clear, I'm not sharing this to discredit special education because that would be foolish and ungrateful.

But a big part of me does believe these teachers are stretched too thin, caught between what they know is right and what the rules require. Over time, the system trains them to follow the process instead of the child. And slowly, their capacity to connect, to respond with creativity or compassion, starts to fade. Not because they don't care, but because the structure doesn't give them the space to show it.

What hurt the most was knowing that Ella was already carrying the weight of being different. She might not have had the words for it, but I'm sure she felt it in the pauses, in the way adults exchanged glances, in how conversations shifted when she entered the room. So when we sat in meetings that were supposed to offer support and instead heard those same exclusionary messages repeated, just dressed up in percentiles and aggregate data, it stirred something in us. Because as her parents, we weren't there to be reminded of what she lacked. We were there to discover what inspires her, and to use that light to help guide her forward. We needed people beside us who could see the child beyond the paperwork. People who were willing to believe in her, and devoted enough to help us rewrite the narrative.

Breakaway

I wasn't a special education teacher, but I was once a credentialed teacher in my own right. I taught sixth grade in a low-income neighborhood in Sacramento. I was young and ambitious, and I walked into that classroom every day knowing I was lucky to be there, to be trusted with that kind of responsibility. So, I gave it everything I had.

Even then, there was always more to do, more attention those students needed, and more time I could've devoted to them. But the days were long, the resources were thin, and the pay barely made it all sustainable. What kept me going was how much I cared about those students and their experiences during such an important phase of their development. And I know most teachers feel the same way. I believe we all do it because we care.

That's why I've written this book with both empathy and honesty. I know how hard the job can be, but I also know what it feels like to be on the other side now. To be the parent of a student with special needs who depends on that educational system. And the truth is, the system has to change and evolve. Because despite the progress we've made in the last handful of decades, students like Ella are still being consistently overlooked and hugely underestimated.

We can't keep pretending that good intentions are enough, and that morality alone will close the gap. We need systems that reflect the same belief in our students with special needs that we carry for their typical peers. And we have to understand that we're all better off as a society when all students are given the chance to reach their fullest potential.

Ella deserves more. They all deserve more. And it's time we start making it happen.

There has always been a quiet contrast between us and most other families. At family gatherings, in parks, in everyday moments, the difference in our lived experiences stood out. Not just with strangers, but even with those closest to us. We watched as other newborns progressed with ease, hitting milestones we were still working toward. Feeding came much more naturally. Sleep was less interrupted. The rhythm of daily life looked smoother, more predictable. Not necessarily easier in every sense, but undeniably less complicated than ours.

It was impossible not to notice. And it wasn't out of envy, but it was just the reality of things. They had their lives and we had ours. And while every child is different, the contrast was sharp. As Ella grew year over year, those differences only deepened. Her path was slower, heavier, shaped by systems and surroundings that made everything more difficult than it needed to be.

We have friends whose children are the same age as Ella. They're all in high school now, finding independence, joining clubs, and stepping into the edges of adulthood. And yet, Ella's experience continues to be constrained by a world that was never built with her in mind. That's the truth most people never see. The systems, the timelines, the expectations were never designed for students with special needs. So every step forward takes more time. Every small breakthrough is hard-earned. And every barrier must be questioned, challenged, and sometimes rebuilt from the ground up. We live with that contrast every day.

As we began contemplating pre-K, we found ourselves sitting with the subdued but unmistakable insights that had gradually taken shape. They began to guide our conversations and influence the directions we were leaning toward. We talked often, sometimes late into the night, aware that we were standing at a true crossroads. We understood how important this next step would be, the beginning of Ella's formal education, and we felt the weight of getting it right. At the same time, we knew just how little we truly understood about the educational system or what the future might demand of us.

In the end, we didn't choose out of clarity. We chose because we believed she deserved a real chance. It was an act of hope, grounded in the fundamental truth we had come to accept. If we wanted something different for Ella, we couldn't keep walking the same path. Even as newcomers, we could already tell where that road would lead.

Through a ton of research and countless conversations with other parents, we eventually discovered a small private school tucked away in East Palo Alto that offered something close to what we'd been searching for. It was called Hope Technology School, and from the moment we arrived, it felt different, like it had actually been created with someone like Ella in mind.

Just outside the classroom doors were spaces for movement and gathering, therapy rooms designed for physical and occupational support, and quiet spaces carved out for individual work or small group learning. It wasn't just a school. It was an environment for learning shaped with intention.

Sending Ella to Hope was not a decision we made lightly. It came with real costs. Financially, it was well beyond what we could reasonably afford at the time. We were still building our careers, trying in vain to steady our startup roles while juggling the constant demands of family life. Every month required extra effort and every paycheck was stretched to the limit. But we happily sacrificed anyway, because we believed that the right environments would shape the course of her life.

The school itself told a story. Its layout, its culture, its atmosphere, it all pointed toward something rare. A place where students were meant to be seen, supported, and celebrated. Here, children with and without disabilities learn side by side. The diversity was more than visual. It was cultural and personal, and it was woven into the very fabric of daily life. We saw students from every background laughing in the hallways, working together in classrooms, and showing us what real inclusion could look like.

Though it felt like the kind of place that could hold our daughter's full identity, it wasn't just the design of the building that moved us. It was the people who brought inclusion to life inside of that building. The staff radiated warmth. Every teacher and support specialist we met was focused, attentive, and genuinely joyful.

They weren't burned out or rushing through conversations for the sake of more paperwork. Instead, they were present, and more than anything, they seemed excited to be part of Ella's journey. That energy alone was enough to make us believe we had finally found a place ready to meet her with the same sense of purpose and possibility we carried every day.

All that being said, the logistics layered on top of financial struggles made things even more difficult. The school was tucked into a corner of East Palo Alto that required a toll bridge crossing just to reach on time. That meant early mornings and slow drives through the crush of Bay Area traffic. It meant always leaving work early to make it in time for pickup, crawling through a sea of brake lights to get back home at a reasonable time.

Yes, we gave up time and comfort. And, we gave up the sense of ease that many other families seemed to take for granted, especially when we could've driven five minutes to multiple schools in our area. Even now, with years of distance and hindsight, I can say for certain that I'd make the same choice again. It may not have worked out in the long run, and it did ask so much of our family in the interim, but when it came down to offering Ella that kind of an opportunity, the choice was simple.

What confirmed everything, and what will always make it one of our best decisions, were Ella's teachers during her time at Hope. They were nothing short of extraordinary. Not just as educators, but as caring and empathetic human beings. Both of them shared the same pre-K classroom, and from the very beginning, they treated Ella as if she were their own. They saw her. They celebrated her, and they supported her in ways that have fundamentally shaped the person she is today.

Every morning, I would drop her off and feel a sense of peace. I knew she was safe. I knew she was in the right place at that moment in time, and for that I'm eternally grateful.

Breakaway

From the very beginning, even before she was born, we knew this life wasn't going to just happen on its own. The moment we learned about Ella's condition, and all that it would take just to keep her alive, the surgeries, the interventions, the constant monitoring, it hit us that nothing about this journey was going to be easy. Her life wasn't something that would simply unfold. It would need to be built, step by step. It would need to be fought for.

I don't know if that changed how I saw myself as a parent, because honestly, this was the only version of parenthood I'd ever known. There was no before. There was only this, a sense of duty that felt immediate and heavy but also deeply personal. Somehow it felt like I was placed here for a reason. Moving mountains for her wasn't just what I had to do, it felt like what I was meant to do, long before I even understood what love or sacrifice really meant.

Very early in the journey, we met with a military chaplain who told us that Ella was meant to be our daughter, and we were meant to be her parents. At the time, those words felt hollow. I held onto them for years, unsettled by the idea that this was destiny. What kind of fate was that, for her or for us? What had she done to enter a world filled with such challenge, and what had we done to deserve a weight like that?

It didn't make sense to me then. But now, it does.

Now I understand what that chaplain was trying to say. Ella wasn't placed in our lives by chance. She was ours because we were the ones who would rise, the ones who would build, advocate, and believe. We were the ones who would keep showing up, no matter how uncertain the path. Because she was always meant to be ours, and we were always meant to be hers, bound together in a love that was never accidental but always essential, the kind of love that shapes a family and gives life its truest meaning.

CHAPTER 5

WORDS THAT MATTER

Looking back, I realize I'd been moving toward this moment long before I ever stepped into an IEP meeting or began to reckon with the inequalities of education. The signs were there, subtle but insistent, pointing me toward a road I didn't yet have the language to name. What I felt was a pull toward something more real, more human, something that asked me to live with intention. I wanted my life to matter, and deep down I knew that meaning would only be found in work that felt true. Teaching, as it turned out, wasn't just part of the journey. It was the beginning of a calling that would change everything.

But clarity doesn't always arrive the way you expect. Sometimes it comes through tension, through words that unsettle, through moments you wish had never happened. In fact, two months after I'd graduated from Davis, on a normally quiet and forgettable Thursday evening, my father said some things I wish I'd never heard. Hurtful words that came from the same man who had once fled across the world in search of a better life. The man who delivered pizzas in the rain to make ends meet, long before he fully understood the English language, and at a time when folded paper maps were the only guide.

He used to tell us stories about driving that old Ford Maverick through the affluent streets of Palo Alto, searching for street signs in the dark as the minutes ticked away. During those days, Domino's promised that your pizza would arrive in less than thirty minutes or it'd be free. So when time ran out, drivers like my father made no money, and he'd hear words from complete strangers that a grown man, providing for his family, should never hear. It was incredibly unethical to manipulate employees like that, but then again, it was the America of the 1980s.

On that particular night I decided to share a decision I'd been wrestling with throughout my entire college experience. After a dismal introduction to organic chemistry, I had long since abandoned the path toward medical school, and though law seemed like a viable option, it never really spoke to me as a long term career. What I truly wanted in that idealistic and utopian mind of mine was an attempt at changing the world, on my own terms.

All along I'd been told by classmates and teachers alike, including the grey-bearded Mr. Greer from Geometry, that I had a knack for sharing information. There was something about presenting that brought joy to my life instead of fear. It was evident in the way I instinctively leveraged that old Macintosh to create lessons and how I'd always present with such ease.

What changed everything for me was the day I discovered a little-known major called Community and Regional Development and a potential career focused on improving lives at scale. I knew I'd never take another chemistry class again. I was fascinated by the power of possibility, stories of communities both falling apart and coming together, and most of all the Asian American experience. I started working with community leaders, became the founding President of an on-campus organization, and I began leading change within the neighborhoods of nearby Sacramento.

Deciding on a career, I felt the urge to follow what authentically meant the most, fueled by the likes of Jaime Escalante in *Stand and Deliver*, and keen on becoming the kind of educator that Mrs. Bigelow, one of my earliest champions, always believed I could be. It was a universal calling too strong to be ignored. So I shared with my father the decision to pursue a career in teaching.

Remember those words I never should've heard? They described how worthless I'd become to our family, how I'd made such a selfish decision to waste my college degree, and how everything he'd ever done to build our future had been lost on me. He asked why I'd ever want to teach. Why would anyone go to college in the first place, if this was to be the goal?

Turns out, in making a selfless and noble decision to teach, I'd shattered his life-long dream for me. And in the eyes of a father born in another place and time, choosing this path meant I'd be nothing more than an embarrassment to the family. It was a lot to work through, so for almost a year we didn't speak, even when I came home to see the rest of my family. Because at that point there were no words left to say. I'd already heard things that a son, who'd always tried to make his father proud, should never hear.

I'm not sure whether it was the immediate desperation that demanded strength, or the eternal underdog in me that refused to stand down. But the motivation to carve out my own narrative became so much stronger after the falling-out with my father. I drove off that night with no intention of ever looking back, with only a hamper full of clothes, a few hundred bucks to my name, and literally no place to stay, except for a few worn-down couches that belonged to some college friends.

Fast forward a few years and I found myself standing in front of a sixth grade classroom. I was disciplining a young lady seemingly out of control and completely at odds with what I believed a student should be. She was loud, obnoxious, rebellious and engaging all at the same time. Eleven going on twenty-five, and as fate would have it, assigned to me. Her name was Priscilla, and it was my first day at Glenwood Elementary.

Fortunately for me, between the emotional departure from home and the morning I met Priscilla, I had the privilege of meeting one of the greatest guides of my life. His name was Dr. Donald Fuller, a former Peace Corp member from the 70s and owner of the baddest F350 diesel truck I'd ever seen. He was the kind of person who looks you directly in the eye, and with very little reservation, tells you exactly how he feels. The kind of school principal who interviews you once, then calls a few weeks later to offer you an opportunity that would change your life.

It was one of those vanilla-colored wall phones that hung in the kitchen with an extra-long curly cord. I was completely taken by surprise when it rang that evening, and in the span of just a few seconds, the conversation started feeling surreal. Dr. Fuller was on the other end, explaining how much potential there was to guide these young students, and how the fact that I was a first-generation immigrant would resonate so well with students from similar backgrounds. He was offering a full-time, sixth grade teaching position at Glenwood Elementary, and I was completely blown away.

What I hadn't yet come to grips with though, was just how demanding that opportunity would turn out to be. There was something about teaching that felt respectable, even honorable, at least on the surface. But inside those classroom walls, the reality was far more complicated. Many of my students came from low-income households where food was sometimes hard to come by, where they didn't always have a steady place to live, and where generational trauma was deep-seated and difficult to understand.

They brought those realities with them to school, not because they wanted to, but because they had no other choice. So I became more than just their teacher. I was a surrogate parent at times taking them to basketball games and fishing trips, a counselor when they needed someone to talk to, and an advocate for the family outside of classroom walls.

And while the responsibilities were immense, the compensation made life difficult. It felt like a cruel irony that the people entrusted with shaping the future could barely afford to secure their own. Most of us didn't have side gigs because there were too few hours outside of the classroom, but the expectations still weighed on us.

It became so intense that one of my fellow teachers was arrested for drunk driving during our lunch break, on a school day. While it shocked us to hear the news, it also didn't. The pressure was relentless and the emotional toll was entirely unspoken. Yet the system continued to move forward, and we still showed up each morning, still believing in the promise of education and doing our best to help bring up these students.

Breakaway

I remained a school teacher for two remarkable years, sending my students to the seventh grade as prepared as I could and with the greatest of intentions. Those years were short-lived, but they became a turning point I'll never forget. Teaching was a confluence of adventure, conflict, and gratitude, the kind of career that leaves its mark whether you like it or not.

What I discovered was that teaching wasn't the dreamlike calling I had once imagined. It wasn't all rainbows and butterflies. It was long nights of lesson planning, mornings that started before sunrise, and afternoons where exhaustion met responsibility. It was joy and heartbreak sitting in the same classroom, often in the same hour.

And yet, it was also deeply formative, because it showed me that meaning doesn't come from ease. It comes from standing in the middle of the work, even when it's messy, and choosing to keep showing up.

Looking back, I realize how audacious that part of my life truly was because I was willing to try, willing to step into a role that demanded more than I thought I had to give. Teaching taught me something I still hold close.

Turned out that listening to my inner voice and choosing

to veer off in pursuit of something greater wasn't a bad idea after all.

Years later, I found myself on the other side of the classroom door. Not as a young teacher this time, but as the father of a little girl starting her very own journey of discovery. I always knew Hope Technology was a beginning for Ella and not the end all, be all. It was a sanctuary when we needed one, a place where she could grow, be seen, and belong. But as she entered her elementary school years, it became clear that we would need to revisit public education. Not because we had given up on the idea of inclusion or that we had a renewed sense of confidence in the system, but because we now had the capacity to be more involved, to potentially expand her life beyond the walls of a small, secluded private school.

Ella was ready as well. She'd developed a growing comfort with routines, a blossoming interest in the world around her, and the kind of joyful curiosity that made new environments feel adventurous. Her affection for stories, her fascination with animals and textures, her ability to remember familiar faces and favorite places were telling developmental markers. They were early glimpses of the person she was becoming and so we approached the transition with the same faith we'd carried since the start.

Her early grade school years brought with them a mix of encouragement and complexity. From the very beginning, she was placed with teachers who approached her with warmth, patience, and optimism. Each morning she walked into the classroom with a smile, eager to greet the adults she trusted and the classmates whose names she quickly learned. She responded well to structure, found comfort in routine, and began to develop in the various environments she was privy to.

Of course, there were many hard days as well. Growth and struggle often travel together, and Ella brought her whole self to school, her brilliance, her humor, her sensitivity, and oftentimes her intensity. Her teachers and paraeducators carried a weight that few outside the classroom truly understand. There were stretches of time when my phone rang almost daily, receiving calls and voicemails from the front office. Sometimes it was a simple check-in to reassure us that she was okay despite an incident in class. Sometimes it was a plea to console her over the phone. And other times, it was a request to take her home altogether.

There are moments I can't shake like the time she scratched one of her best friends on the bus, leaving a huge scar below his eye. The many afternoons when she refused to leave the playground, anchoring her body with all her might, her entire class waiting. The heartbreaking episodes when she laid on the classroom floor or under her desk, inconsolable, crying out from a place she couldn't explain.

If it hadn't been for one teacher in particular who just cared so much, for the better part of three years, we don't know where we'd be today. She met Ella's hardest days with a calm that felt like shelter, a kind of grace you learn only through personal experience and heartache. And when the world turned upside down during the pandemic, she somehow steadied it.

There were days of Zoom calls that barely held Ella's attention, moments of confusion when routines disappeared, and long stretches where the isolation felt endless. But even through a screen, this teacher reached her. She continued teaching with empathy and intention, and reminded Ella that school was still a place she belonged, even if it looked different for a while.

When school resumed in person, Ella still carried the strain of those disrupted years. Her regulation was fragile, her transitions harder than before. But her teacher didn't flinch. She adjusted, re-centered, and would relentlessly try again. She reimagined lessons on the fly, spoke to Ella with the kind of language that calms, and found creative ways to bring her back into the moment. When the day ended, she often stayed behind to think deeply about how tomorrow could be better. And when she called us at home, it wasn't always about what went wrong. Sometimes, it was simply to share a bright moment or a connection that'd been made.

She reminded us what it looks like when a teacher truly cares. There was nothing flashy about her approach, no grand pronouncements or elaborate strategies. Just a steady commitment to figuring things out. On the days when Ella struggled to settle, she would sit beside her quietly, never rushing, never raising her voice. When the rest of the class moved on, she would stay with Ella, adjusting the lesson, simplifying instructions, sometimes even tossing the plan altogether just to keep her engaged.

What she offered made all the difference in the world. She never made Ella feel like a problem, and she never made us feel like outsiders. She simply stayed in it with us. And in those early years, especially during the chaos and uncertainty of a global pandemic, that kind of steady presence mattered more than anything else. She reminded us that someone else believed in our daughter too.

Breakaway

I sometimes think of my father back in the eighties, standing outside that old blue Maverick, rain falling across his jacket, a map spread on the hood as he tried to make sense of a world that had little space for him. He didn't have the language, the resources, or the support, yet he kept showing up, one delivery at a time, learning how to survive in a country that wasn't built with him in mind.

Decades later, I found myself sitting alone in my own car, just outside a school parking lot, staring through the windshield after yet another tough day in the classroom. I didn't have a map spread before me, but I was just as lost, wondering how I'd keep going when the work felt so heavy. And yet, like him, I stayed. I pushed through the exhaustion, the doubt, the uncertainty, because some part of me believed there was meaning buried in the struggle.

In those quiet moments, I began to see how our lives were connected. His journey and mine were different in detail, but the rhythm was the same. Two people in different times, searching for direction, refusing to give up, holding on to the hope that perseverance itself would one day point us where we were meant to go.

I was beginning to understand that inclusion isn't something you wait for. It isn't granted by systems or sealed in policy. It's created in the ordinary, in the steady rhythm of choices and gestures that seem small but add up to something lasting. It's in the way a teacher kneels down to meet a child at eye level. It's in the way a parent steadies themselves after a long day and chooses to believe again. It's in the willingness to sit through the silence, to hold the line when progress feels far away, to keep seeing the whole person even when the world insists on narrowing them down.

That truth came alive when I taught school. It came alive again with Ella. And slowly, I realized that inclusion isn't just a concept. It's a practice. It's the daily work of love and belief, repeated until the future begins to look different than the past.

And maybe that's the lesson I needed most. That even when the map is unclear and the road ahead is uneven, we can still choose to take the next step. We can still decide to make space, to open doors, to build something better. Inclusion, in the end, isn't about waiting for permission. It's all of us walking forward together, one step at a time, toward a horizon that's yet to be written.

CHAPTER 6
REFUSING TO SETTLE

The summer before middle school brought with it both anticipation and anxiety, at least on my part. We'd made it through the long and often difficult stretch of elementary school, and while that journey had its challenges, we still believed brighter days were ahead. Ella was developing well, and it felt like the right moment to pause, to be grateful for our health and our happiness, and to take in how far we'd come. But even in that space of gratitude, I couldn't avoid the weight of what was coming next.

Seventh grade was just around the corner.

I'm not sure how visible it was on the outside, but inside I was deeply anxious about Ella transitioning to a much bigger school. There would be more students, more noise, and far less predictability. I imagined it would feel overwhelming for her, just as it already felt overwhelming to me. But once again, Ella reminded us that moments like these are never too big for her.

Just as she'd done in elementary school before, she stepped into this new environment with confidence and grace. On that first morning, all I needed to do was ask one of the administrators to walk her to class. From there, she took the lead. She explored the campus, settled into her routine, and made herself at home. Middle school, as it turned out, was hers to claim.

Each morning, she started the day with excitement and purpose, often dancing her way to class, energized by her favorite songs in the car and the comfort of routine. Her friends meant the world to her. She knew them well, talked about them and their families constantly, and was all smiles every time they were together.

The school itself had just begun a major renovation when she arrived, and it looked the part with freshly painted walls, modern structures, and a welcoming atmosphere that felt both current and inviting. Her classroom was spacious, almost like a studio, with a private office and kitchen tucked inside. It was located near the front desk, where staff members got to know her in short order.

It felt like we were doing right by her, giving her a chance to grow in a space that was warm, familiar, and full of possibility. Most importantly, it felt safe. And for that alone, we were deeply grateful.

Even so, something fundamental was missing from this middle school experience, and it never quite came together. Seventh grade had started off with promise, but after just a few months into the year, her special education teacher left without much explanation. I'm fairly certain it had to do with his credentials and certification, but it was never completely transparent to us.

We were just beginning to develop a working relationship, figuring out the best ways to communicate and incrementally share many of Ella's characteristics and tendencies. Instead, a series of substitutes rotated through in his absence, none of them able to stay long enough to establish a rhythm.

While the paraeducator team stayed mostly intact and did their best to keep things steady, the classroom never quite found its rhythm. There was no firm foundation to build upon, and whatever momentum came with each new teacher faded quickly. Academically, the year became a blur.

Ella had adjusted to the school and found comfort in its routines. It became a place she genuinely loved, but the daily work of learning never really took hold. Just thinking about it wore us down. As a family, we found ourselves constantly trying to balance her emotional wellness with any hope of academic progress.

Eventually, in an effort to preserve our own well-being, we let go of the pressure and chose instead to be grateful for what we did have, a daughter who was safe, joyful, and thriving in her own way.

Breakaway

I think it's important to admit that no matter how much love we have for our children, we're still human. We can only push so far before the weight starts to pull us down too. At some point you have to stop measuring progress against the standards set by a system and start asking what your family actually needs in order to stay whole.

For us, that moment came late one night after another long school day. Ella had fallen asleep in her room, still smiling from the music she loved, and her sister was finally down too. My wife and I sat at the table, papers spread out in front of us, the same data we'd been told to obsess over. Neither of us said much at first. We just looked at each other and knew we couldn't keep chasing numbers that never told the whole story of who our daughter was.

So, we decided to protect our own sanity and give ourselves permission to rest in the joy of who Ella was, not just in what she was learning.

There's no shame in that, and there shouldn't be. Because the truth is, if we burn ourselves out trying to meet expectations that were never built with our children in mind, we risk losing the very strength they depend on most. Sometimes the bravest thing you can do is step back, breathe, and remember that joy itself is progress.

By eighth grade, things had stabilized slightly. Ella had a teacher she truly enjoyed and a classroom that felt more grounded, but the ripple effects from the year before hadn't fully settled. There were still stretches of inconsistency, including another long-term substitute phase. Throughout it all, behavioral issues within the class began to resurface, and it became harder to ignore that Ella wasn't progressing in the ways we'd hoped.

We continued meeting with her teachers and administrators. The conversations were always kind and full of encouragement, but they rarely focused on Ella's academic growth. Most of the attention stayed on her behavior, her social adjustments, and the moments when she showed resistance or frustration, but not on whether she was actually learning.

Looking back, I wonder if it was the unstable environment itself that triggered many of those behaviors. And while I still don't know how much more could've been done, I do have some regret. I wish I had held the district's leadership more accountable for the conditions they allowed to persist.

At home, we began to notice some patterns. The work she brought back looked almost identical to what we'd seen before. Everything felt eerily familiar, the same concepts, same format, same results. It seemed as though the curriculum had stalled, looping through the basics without much progress to show for it. We couldn't tell if she was actually moving forward academically, and it became even harder to pinpoint what was standing in the way.

Was it her ability as a learner? Had we given enough attention to the goals outlined in her IEP, or had we passively surrendered to the system? And more than anything, was the classroom environment helping her grow, or simply containing her?

It wasn't one single moment that told us something wasn't right. It was more of a slow accumulation of small doubts that built over time. And maybe, if we're being honest, we didn't want to face it. We were tired and mentally worn down. Unsure of what to do and just hoping that things might somehow improve on their own. We told ourselves that middle school was almost over, and for better or worse, that became the justification. If we could just make it through, that would be enough for now. So we did, and we let the school year run its course.

By the time eighth grade ended, we found ourselves looking ahead with a renewed sense of focus. High school was next, and with it, new teachers, new routines, and maybe, just maybe, a chance to start again. I've always said that hope isn't much of a strategy. But sometimes, when that's all you have, it's enough to keep going.

Breakaway

Middle school had taken a lot out of us. We were worn down, no question about it. But when summer came, something started to shift. I finally had the space to slow down, to think, and to dive into the research that had been calling me for a while. I was learning how the systems were built, where they fell short, and how families like ours were too often left on the margins. It wasn't just about Ella anymore. It was about connecting the dots, starting to see the bigger picture, and realizing there were ways to push for something better. For the first time in a long time, my mind felt clear, and my energy came back. That summer gave me exactly what I needed, perspective, focus, and a sense that maybe high school could be different. Thank goodness it came when it did.

During the early summer months, as we began preparing for high school, I came across a presentation by the Sacramento County Office of Education and a section in the California Education Code that outlined a promising new possibility. It described an alternative pathway to a high school diploma, one specifically designed for students who benefit from more time, intentional pacing, and personalized support. From everything I read, this wasn't about lowering expectations. It was a standards-based approach that led to the same diploma as any other student, with greater flexibility to meet different needs along the way.

The more I read, the more certain I became. This wasn't just a maybe. In fact, it was the direction we needed to take. I spent the summer gathering information, reviewing policy documents, highlighting key sections, and organizing everything in a way that felt clear and compelling. It felt like I was building something solid and tangible that others could stand behind. As soon as the school year began, I submitted a formal request for an IEP meeting and sent all the materials in advance. I felt ready. I believed we were presenting a thoughtful, student-centered plan that deserved a real response.

Walking into that meeting, I carried a strong sense of purpose. I knew what we were asking for, and I believed in the preparation that had brought us there. This felt like the beginning of something important, and more so, a chance to build shared commitment around helping Ella earn her diploma. We knew she was capable of learning and growing with the right support. All we hoped was that the team could see it too, and take the next step with us toward a future that honored her potential as both a student and a full participant in the world around her.

Unfortunately, what followed was a deflating departure from the hope and optimism we'd brought forth. From the very beginning, the tone of the meeting felt misaligned. There was no real curiosity. No shared sense of possibility. The team responded with caution. They questioned whether Ella even qualified, despite the clear alignment between the guidelines we presented and her needs. They pointed to moot points and outdated criteria, as if expecting us to back down in the face of process and policy. And most disappointing of all, they spoke in vague terms about what high school might look like for her, offering soft reassurances rather than concrete plans. The gap between their expectations and what we knew Ella was capable of was undeniable, and their version of success fell far short of the future we were fighting for.

We pushed back. We pointed directly to the code, to the language written with students like Ella in mind. But the tone in the room never changed. It was clear that no one had seriously considered what we were proposing. There was no meaningful dialogue. No next steps. Just polite resistance wrapped in procedure. We were told this wasn't how things were usually done, that it would require too many adjustments, that Ella's path was already headed in a different direction.

And then came the moment I still think about. One of her teachers, while trying to offer a glimpse of what success might look like, suggested that maybe Ella could one day work at the local drugstore. There was no malice in the comment, and it wasn't said with cruelty, but the vision was incredibly narrow. So narrow that it became impossible to ignore. That was the moment the scale tipped. The moment we knew we had to walk a different path. We had spent years believing in her potential, watching her overcome challenge after challenge. There was no way we were going to stop now.

We didn't walk into that meeting to pick a fight. We came because we believed in our daughter's future and hoped to partner with a team that could see it too. But when the conversation shifted from what was possible to what wasn't, I knew we were in the wrong room.

One of the last steps I took before stepping away was reaching out to a special education attorney based in Los Angeles. He'd worked with families like ours before and understood the complexities of the law. He was direct and clear, and told us he was willing to take on our case. From a legal standpoint, we had every reason to move forward. Ella met the criteria. The education code supported our request. And if we filed a suit, we would likely have a strong case.

But then he asked me something that just made so much sense. What would this battle really achieve? What would Ella gain and what might she lose? He wasn't talking about money. He was talking about time, focus, and emotional weight. These types of lawsuits are long and invasive, and they are rarely transformational in the ways people hope. It could take months, maybe longer, just to get a hearing. And all that time, Ella would be waiting, not learning, and not growing. She'd just be stuck in a system that had already moved on without her.

I sat with that question for a long time, long after the call ended. I thought about the toll it would take on our family. I thought about what Ella might feel if she sensed us locked in a battle she never asked for. I tried to imagine the weight of legal proceedings, procedural delays, letters, deadlines, and denials on top of everything else. And I couldn't ignore the truth. Even if we won on paper, the cost would be far greater than the reward because she'd be the one living through it. She'd be the one held in place while the adults fought around her. And if we finally reached the outcome we wanted, what would be left of her joy, her trust, and her love of learning?

That conversation stayed with me and it ultimately clarified what mattered. We weren't afraid to fight. We simply chose not to lose her in the process.

Still, walking away was not easy, especially not for Ella. She asked about school constantly. She asked about her classmates, her teachers, her favorite aides. She wondered why we weren't driving to school each morning like before. Her joy for that school community had been real. Her excitement, her friendships, her place in that environment all mattered deeply to her. And when it was gone, she felt it.

We did our best to explain, gently and simply, that her learning would look a little different now. That she would still have school, just in another way. But she was still confused and the only way forward was to literally show her what we meant. She knew something had changed, even if she couldn't quite say it, and it broke our hearts every time she asked about her class. It still does till this day.

Breakaway

Too often, families stay quiet because the system makes questioning feel like confrontation. We tell ourselves it's not the right time, that maybe we don't have all the facts, that pushing too hard might close doors rather than open them. So we wait. We hope. We give the benefit of the doubt.

And when progress doesn't come, we adjust our expectations instead of challenging the process. We tell ourselves that stability is enough, that being safe is the same as being supported. But deep down, we know the difference. We know when something is missing.

The truth is, most systems aren't built to stretch. They're simply built to replicate. They reward compliance, not creativity. They favor predictability, not possibility. And when your child doesn't fit neatly into that mold, you're basically left with two choices. It's either you adapt to the system or dare to reimagine it.

Growth is neither polite nor patient. And, it certainly doesn't wait for policy to catch up. Sometimes, believing in your child means breaking with what's familiar. It means trusting that your discomfort may be the very thing that leads to transformation. It can indeed be heartbreaking, but this is what it means to refuse to settle. And, it's not because you're difficult or that you unreasonably expect too much. But because you see what's possible, and you're willing to walk toward it, even if you have to build the road yourself.

So we chose the harder path. We stepped away from a place she loved because we believed she was meant for more. We did it knowing she would grieve that change, and knowing we would grieve it too. But we also did it with conviction, because we believe Ella is meant to live a life of purpose, challenge, joy, and progress. A life that deserves to unfold on her own terms, not within someone else's limited frame.

In the end, the road ahead did narrow, but we didn't wait for permission to find another. We stepped forward and began to build it ourselves, guided by a quiet but unshakable faith in who she was becoming.

And here's the truth I keep coming back to. Every time a family like ours refuses to settle, the ground beneath us shifts. And in those shifts, no matter how small, new roads begin to open. Roads that lead not only to possibility for our own children, but to horizons that generations after us will one day walk.

CHAPTER 7
OPENING PANDORA'S BOX

To share a thought is to risk being seen. Because once you choose, as Pandora once did, to lift the lid, what escapes can be overwhelming. It can shift the air around you. It can change the way people see you, and it could potentially change everything.

For a long time now, I've thought about how silence can start to feel like safety. It wasn't something we were told outright, but it was always there, woven into how we moved through the world. An unspoken understanding that speaking up could conjure risk, that drawing attention might unravel what little stability we had. Over time, I began to wonder how that belief took such a strong hold on our family's way of life. How a story as old as the Greeks, the warning not to lift the lid, not to disturb what lies beneath, impacted how we negotiated the Asian American landscape.

It might sound like an outdated stereotype to some, but for me, it was the reality of things. We were raised to lower our voices. We were encouraged to avoid confrontation, especially when doing so made things more uncomfortable. And, we learned to keep our heads down, to hold our troubles close, and to keep going without making things more complicated.

It's not exactly something I'm proud of, but I do understand how it came to be this way, and it all started back in Vietnam where I was born, a few years after the war ended. But to make sense of my own story, I have to begin with his.

On what I imagine was a heavy, humid evening along the banks of the Mekong River, my father fled the land that raised him. He left behind a family he loved, including a newborn son, and the only life he'd ever known. The decades-long war had ended, but peace had never arrived. So, in search of a future that was solely made of hopes and dreams, he boarded a battered cargo ship, escaped to Malaysia, and eventually took his first flight to the suburbs of Detroit. From there, after a long ride on a Greyhound bus, he found his way to the sunlit edges of Northern California. This was where he began rebuilding his life.

Here by the Bay, he gave up the language that had shaped his thoughts, the cadence and tone that once carried his stories, and traded it for a version of English that never quite let him say what he meant. His sentences came slower, his words more cautious, and so much of what he truly felt was left unspoken. He gave up the comfort of familiar faces around the dinner table and the contentment of home-cooked meals. In its place were strange grocery aisles filled with foods he'd never seen, frozen dinners wrapped in small cardboard boxes, and generic cans of yellow corn with labels that were always lost in translation.

But still, he pressed on. He learned one word at a time, stumbling through small conversations, picking up bits of language from coworkers, cashiers, and bus drivers who tolerated his presence. He adjusted his way of life, found new ways to make ends meet, and discovered small comforts in unfamiliar places. Even in a world that never fully saw him, he stayed. He worked. He built a life the only way he knew how, through effort, repetition, and the dignity of showing up every single day.

In time, he learned how to survive, and came to understand that more than anything, his livelihood rested on the shoulders of silence. Given the imposing language barrier, you spoke only when spoken to. You didn't question authority. You worked hard, studied harder, and kept your head down so you wouldn't draw attention. As paradoxical as it sounds, the easiest way to belong was to stay unnoticed.

It'd be a few years before my mother and I would make our way out of Vietnam, by way of our own miraculous journey, holding on to the belief that we'd see him again.

When we finally arrived in the United States, the virtually impossible reunion was finally complete. Not only did all three of us manage to escape the communist regime, but we somehow found each other on the other side of the world.

Fast forward a few decades and it turned out that living beneath the shadows of Silicon Valley had given my parents their American dream. They managed to buy a home in a place they'd once only imagined. My brother and I eventually went to college, earned our degrees, started families, and found our own ways to give back. Aside from a few details, this was the outcome they'd been chasing all along; and naturally, it became the path we were expected to follow. It called for discipline, for humility, and for a steady kind of resilience that never asked for more than what was given.

But every dream carries a cost, and theirs was no different. The life they built taught us to bury our troubles, and to silence our voices. "Keep your head down. Work hard. Don't cause trouble." That was my father's refrain ever since I can remember. And for a long time, I believed that silence kept us safe, that staying unseen was the most reliable way to build something lasting.

However, as my world became incrementally larger, that silence began to take on a different shape. What once felt like safety began to feel like surrender, and there came a point when going along with the currents no longer felt passive, but complicit. When saying nothing started to feel like saying it was okay. That shift unfolded slowly through many lived experiences and a more mature sensibility about how the world works. And as I navigated through my own difficulties and saw for myself what life and living truly demanded, I began to let go of the script I'd inherited. There was a voice inside of me, one I'd spent years learning to understand, that started to demand more of my attention.

It was the same voice I've since learned to trust with everything I have.

At long last, I gave myself permission to speak the truth. Not to be noticed, and not because I had everything figured out, but because I believed the stories deserved to be told. I began as a community advocate, standing beside immigrant families whose hopes often went unheard. Then as an educator, believing that learning could change lives, and that I could be part of the ultimate solution. I've also spoken as a veteran, as someone who had worn this nation's uniform with pride, and who still believes in the promise of service.

And perhaps most importantly, I began speaking as a father who sees in his daughter a future full of light, purpose, and possibility. Her life, like every life, is worth showing up for. And sharing my honest perspective, especially when it's uncomfortable, has become part of how I honor that.

Now I find myself at another inflection point, one that feels just as personal, but shaped by a different kind of urgency. This time, it's no longer about reclaiming or developing my own voice. It's about walking alongside Ella as she begins to discover hers. It's about choosing to lift that lid as many times as needed, believing in her and in the fact that students like her deserve so much more than just proximity or permission. They deserve an entire future that sees them fully.

Today, as I'm writing these words, that belief seems to matter more than ever. We're living in a moment when the very systems that were created to support our students are beginning to fracture, when the language of equity is spoken often but carried out unevenly, and when inclusion, once held up as a promise, is increasingly treated as optional. This is certainly not a time for silence.

This is a time to speak with clarity, to act with purpose, and to insist on something better for those who have waited long enough. This book is ultimately about what becomes possible when we speak with purpose, when we stand beside those who are still learning to trust their voice, and when we step forward with strength, even when the path ahead is still unfolding.

You know, there's a part of Pandora's story that many people don't realize. After all the struggle had been released into the world, after every hardship had taken its place, one thing still remained inside the box.

That something was hope.

Breakaway

The truth is, I carry a lot with me. I'm the son of refugees who gave up everything just to start again. I'm Asian American, raised with the unspoken rule that keeping your head down was the safest way to move forward. I'm a veteran who believed in service, and still does. I'm an educator who believes people can grow, even when the systems around them say otherwise. And I'm a father, a deeply proud one, who's learning how to show up in the ways that matter most.

I take all of those intersectional identities into a room with me when I speak. They shape the questions I ask, the silences I refuse, and the words I choose to put down on paper. They remind me that voice isn't just sound. It's lineage. It's experience. It's responsibility.

And that's why this all feels so personal. Because once you've seen how things really are, and how much better they could be, you don't get to pretend anymore. You don't get to sit quietly and hope someone else will fix it. You either step forward, or you step aside.

I didn't grow up expecting to challenge schools or any institution for that matter. I was taught to respect them, to trust that they were fair, and to believe that good people doing meaningful work would naturally do what was right. And maybe that was true in theory, but over time, the cracks became harder to ignore. At first, I blamed what most people do, overcrowded classrooms, shrinking budgets, professionals doing their best with far too much on their plates. But eventually, I began to see it for what it was. This was not just a system that was burdened. It was a system that had learned to stay quiet.

I saw it in the stories of other families. I heard it in their voices. I felt it in my own experience. And through it all, a pattern kept emerging. We're part of a structure that depends on politeness, expects deference, and assumes families like ours will stay thankful for whatever is offered.

The silence never announces itself. It simply becomes part of the process, woven into the routines and phrases we're expected to accept. Phrases like "let's wait and see" or "we're doing the best we can," made it harder to speak without feeling like you were breaking some unspoken rule. And for those of us who were raised to believe that speaking up might come at a cost, it was easy to let that silence settle in, to believe it was the proper path forward.

But my father's journey showed me what it means when those with the least power are asked to be the most patient. I've seen how silence gets framed as cooperation, how the lowest of expectations are recast as realistic goals, how the way forward becomes so dim that you begin to forget there was ever any light at all.

In our communities, particularly among Asian American, immigrant, and refugee families, silence was not always a choice made freely. As was the case with my own family, it's oftentimes passed down, something taught not because it was ideal, but because it once served a purpose. It kept someone safe and protected them from harm. It allowed them to survive in a world that was never built to receive them.

My father understood that better than most. In fact, he lived with the awareness that his presence in this country came with conditions, that being accepted often meant being quiet, that being respected often meant being unseen. He carried that burden without complaint. His strength was not in what he said, but in how he endured. He provided for us with a steady hand and a quiet heart, and he did so while making sure we understood what it meant to live as guests in a place that was never designed with us in mind. In doing so, he didn't raise his voice or challenge authority because he had learned the cost of being too visible. And in the way he loved and protected us, he passed along those lessons with care, believing it was the best way to help us build this American life.

As a young man, I admired him for that, and I still do. The relentless strength he carried, the way he moved through the world without complaint, the steadiness with which he provided for our family, all of it taught me what it means to endure with dignity. But over time, I've come to understand that the silence that protected him, the restraint that helped him survive, is not what my daughter needs now. Because silence, even when wrapped in grace and humility, still has the power to diminish. It causes you to doubt your own instincts. It somehow makes lowered expectations sound reasonable. And perhaps most harmful of all, it deceivingly dresses up limitations as kindness.

I never wanted to be difficult, never wanted to be the one who pushed too hard or asked too many questions. I believed for a long time that it was better to stay respectful, better to stay grateful, better to go along with the people who were supposed to know best. But when it came to Ella, I just couldn't pretend that deference was still serving us. I'd seen what happened when we allowed others to define what was realistic. I'd watched as potential was reframed as naivety, as ambition was met with polite warnings, as systems designed to reward compliance slowly reshaped our dreams into something smaller and more manageable.

And so I began building a very different path. Not with anger, and not to provoke, but because I could no longer carry the silence that had shaped so much of my upbringing. I stopped softening my questions. I stopped apologizing for wanting more. I started asking for clarity, challenging the narrative, and calling things what they were. Because speaking up doesn't always have to come with volume or fire. Sometimes it's just the steady act of standing in front of those who hold power over your child's future and refusing to let them speak on your behalf. Sometimes it's about holding space for your truth to be heard clearly, without hesitation. Amazingly enough, something powerful happens in that space. Hope begins to breathe. And when hope has room to breathe, it grows.

I still carry my father's story with me. His tireless work ethic, his unwavering love for our family, and the quiet strength he held through every uncertain moment of life. I carry all of that with deep gratitude, knowing it shaped me in the most fundamentally important ways. But the belief that silence will set you free, well that part ends with me.

Breakaway

Ella has never asked for anything extraordinary. What she wants, and what she deserves, is what every child should be able to count on. To be included, to learn, and to belong. But I've come to understand that even asking for something that simple can feel like too much, especially when the people across the table have already made up their minds about who your child is and how far she'll go.

The truth is, those meetings aren't really about paperwork or procedures. They're about power. They're about who gets to decide what a child's future is supposed to look like, who gets to set the limits and call them realistic, who gets to draw the line between what's possible and what's out of reach. And for families like ours, that power is rarely in our hands. So when we ask for inclusion, when we ask for the same opportunities every other child receives without question, it's not a small request. It's a declaration that our children deserve more than someone else's lowered expectations.

Ella has taught me that belonging isn't a privilege reserved for the few. It's a birthright. It's as essential as air, as natural as breath. And when systems try to ration it, when institutions act as though belonging must be earned, it's our job to remind them that inclusion is not theirs to give or withhold. It's already written into the very dignity of every child who walks through those doors.

So I keep speaking, even when it's uncomfortable. I speak because silence never built anything worth keeping. I speak because Ella deserves a future that is not measured by someone else's doubt, but by the fullness of who she is. And I speak because I know there are other families sitting quietly in those same rooms, waiting for someone to show that it can be done.

Ella isn't asking for anything extraordinary. She's asking for what every child should already have, the chance to be seen, the chance to grow, and the chance to belong. And if that still sounds like too much, then maybe it's not her we should be questioning. Maybe it's the world around her that still has work to do.

At a certain point, I decided it was time to design our own path forward. A life that doesn't wait for permission or ask for approval. A life where truth is spoken even when silence would be easier. A life that stays open, that stays grounded, that keeps believing hope was never meant to be hidden, but to be lived.

CHAPTER 8
FINDING OUR PLACE

You wouldn't think much of it at first. The building itself sits behind another school, tucked away in the back of a large lot and so easy to miss unless you were looking for it. A small sign out front confirmed we'd found the right place, but like the rest of the school, it drew little attention to itself. Inside, the staff worked in relatively tight spaces, their voices flowing easily from one cubicle to the next. It reminded me of the nonprofit offices I had known over the years, places where resources were limited but the sense of purpose was unmistakable. Cozy, perhaps a little crowded, filled with people doing meaningful work.

Of course, Ella was there with us for that first visit. We all sat down with the Assistant Principal, joined by Ms. Roxie, the incredible tutor who'd guided Ella through middle school and has become one of her favorite people in this world. That morning, she was technically still a tutor, but soon after, she would become Ella's dedicated, full-time teacher, walking this new and unfamiliar path alongside us.

We began with questions. How did things work here? What was their approach to special education? How did the IEP process unfold in their specific setting? Did it follow the same rigid structure we had seen before, or was there space for flexibility and collaboration? We weren't asking for promises, only a chance to move forward without constantly feeling like pushing immovable objects uphill.

She listened with care and responded with calm, deliberate intention, fully present in the conversation. It was clear, and deeply appreciated, that she wasn't there to convince us or put on a performance. Her words carried a grounded confidence, the kind that comes from knowing the system well and understanding how to shape it around the student in front of her.

Most of all, her focus was on what would genuinely help each student move forward, finding the steps that matched their needs and gave them the best chance to grow.

What mattered most to us in that moment was finding people willing to create a path together. We needed those who could balance structure with flexibility and approach the process with thoughtfulness rather than rely on a script. In that first meeting, we saw exactly that, and it gave us hope for the path that lay ahead for Ella.

Breakaway

Let me be clear.

Just because someone holds a title or sits in a position of authority doesn't mean they're the one who'll fight for your child. A badge, a degree, or a contract doesn't guarantee heart. As with any profession, there are folks who clock in, follow the script, and clock out again. They manage the paperwork, attend the meetings, and keep the system running, but they don't step into the fire with you.

What your child deserves is more than compliance. They deserve people who will look past the forms and data points and see the student in front of them. People who believe in growth, not limits. People who will sit beside you when things get hard and still refuse to give up. That kind of commitment can't be faked and it can't be taught in teaching programs. It comes from conviction, from character, from the belief that every child deserves a life of possibility.

As parents, we can't afford to be naive. We have to discern who's truly in it with us and who's just passing through. That takes time, patience, and more trial and error than anyone wants to admit. But here's the truth.

The difference between progress and stagnation, between hope and despair, almost always comes down to the people in the room. And when you find the ones who choose to show up with courage instead of excuses, with conviction instead of compliance, you hold on tight. Because those are the people who help move mountains.

Just a week earlier, at her original high school, the atmosphere could not have been more different. We entered that meeting with months of preparation behind us and a plan that was thoughtful, practical, and grounded in the belief that she could pursue an alternative pathway toward a diploma. We spoke about granting her the same opportunity afforded to every other student, including the chance to fail while attempting to achieve something more. Yet before our words could fully take hold, the response was firm and unyielding. In hindsight, it seemed the plan had been set aside before we even arrived, and the potential we described was undermined and reframed as something unattainable.

When that meeting ended, we walked out together, still trying to piece together the oddity of the situation. On the drive back, our words came in starts and stops, each of us testing thoughts aloud, then rethinking them before they were fully formed. We kept circling the same questions, searching for the language that might make sense of it all. There was an underlying urgency in the way we spoke, an unspoken agreement that this mattered and needed to be figured out.

Fortunately for us, a week was enough for everything to start moving in a new direction. Stepping into Ella's new school, the contrast was immediate, even though nothing about the setting was elaborate. The building was simple and the offices were small. Yet the atmosphere felt open in a way we hadn't experienced for some time. Amazingly enough, there was no urgency to draw boundaries or decide what couldn't be done. Instead, there was room to speak freely, to ask questions, and to imagine what might be possible. The teachers and administrators we met listened with genuine attention, letting the conversation find its own rhythm and leaving space for more to emerge.

It was abundantly clear that this would be more than a small change. After all, this was an independent study charter school, which meant leaving behind the familiar cadence of traditional classrooms for something entirely different. Ella's learning would take place mostly at home, guided each day by Ms. Roxie, with the school acting as a hub for advisory support and connection rather than a daily destination. It was a change in structure, in pace, and in the way we imagined her educational journey.

My biggest concern, and one that I'm still solving for today, was that it placed us even further from an inclusive learning environment. That, in and of itself, was a really difficult consequence to accept; but in that moment, it was crucial to assess the situation and identify what we couldn't live without.

The first few weeks carried a strange kind of uncertainty. Ella still held fast to the rhythm of her previous high school, to the people and places that had become part of her week. In her mind, this new arrangement felt temporary, more like a pause in the journey rather than a new chapter. She asked often about her teachers, her classmates and the routines she knew by heart, and she wanted to know when she'd see them again. These were such genuine questions that came from a sense of longing and a continual reminder of the life she'd abruptly left behind.

The emptiness she felt settled in gradually, coming in waves that seemed to imbue themselves into the rhythm of everyday life. When she asked if she'd be going back, we met her with gentleness, answering in a way that respected her feelings while guiding her toward understanding the changes ahead. It was incredibly difficult knowing we couldn't give her the answers she wanted, so we tried our best to make sure she felt heard and understood.

What steadied this transition and saved us was the familiar presence of Ella's favorite person, Ms. Roxie. In fact, without her, none of this would've come to life and this chapter would not have been written. We'd been very fortunate to have her in Ella's life for years, and her arrival each morning brought a sense of comfort and continuity. Ella would greet her with a smile and a hug that left no doubt about how much this connection meant. From there, their day unfolded with a rhythm all its own. Stories were exchanged, inside jokes retold, bits of the previous day's adventures revisited. They read together, walked together, and shared snacks at the kitchen table. Music filled the room, and sometimes the lesson gave way to dancing, laughter spilling into the air. And woven through it all, almost effortlessly, the learning took shape.

Over time, I began to see Ella change in the gentle, steady way a flower leans toward sunlight. She approached her days with more ease, letting the laughter linger, holding her reading a little longer, and filling our conversations with stories about what she and Ms. Roxie had shared. From my usual spot nearby, close enough to hear yet far enough to give them space, I watched her come alive with curiosity, reading with expression, speaking with confidence, and listening with the kind of focus that grows when a person feels truly safe and seen. The trust between them gave each lesson a sense of possibility and opened space for her to explore, grow, and find joy in the process. It was living proof of what I'd always believed, that empowerment flourishes when the right conditions are present, when trust moves in both directions, when expectations are clear, and when joy is woven into the heart of learning.

The trust and joy that shaped those lessons spilled into the rest of our home. Some days my wife and I both worked from home, and we were all there, including both my parents, Ms. Roxie, and our lively dog who loves to be part of the mix. The house was full of sound and movement, yet the rhythm felt natural and steady. Within it, we could see Ella's happiness growing, her confidence deepening, and her light shining a little brighter each day.

About three months into this new chapter, Ella retook the same assessments she'd completed when she started. The results spoke for themselves. Her reading jumped ahead by multiple grade levels. Her comprehension was sharper, more secure. Even in math, where progress had always come more slowly, she was moving forward with steady gains. But the most important shift of all couldn't be measured on paper. It was in her presence, her posture, her tone, her willingness to step into the work without hesitation. She looked more sure of herself. She moved through lessons with a confidence that was rooted not in perfection, but in the knowledge that she was capable and supported.

There was nothing mysterious about it, no hidden formula waiting to be uncovered. What changed was the belief in herself, the behaviors that were guided by a renewed sense of success, and the environment that surrounded her. She had time to move at her own pace and space to explore without being rushed. She was supported by a teacher who arrived each day with patience, consistency, and genuine belief in her abilities.

She knew she could try, stumble, and try again, and that her place would remain hers no matter the outcome.

Even now, Ella will sometimes refer to herself as a student at her former high school, forgetting that she's been somewhere new for almost a year. I'm okay with it because those memories are still hers, and I understand why. I'm happy she's got such great memories from that part of her high school experience, and there are times I wish she could have both, the community she loved and the learning environment where she now flourishes. I know that'll come soon though, because that's what I'm working on each and every day.

For now, it's enough to know that sometimes the place you need most is the one you create for yourself.

Breakaway

I remember distinctly how my heart broke every time she asked about seeing her former classmates. The way she admired and cared for them was so pure, and it cut deeply to know I had made a decision that took her away from that community. I always believed it was the right choice for her and trusted that with time, she'd come to find joy in this new space. But knowing it was right didn't make it easy. It remains one of the hardest things I've ever done on her behalf.

Here's the part most people don't talk about. Doing right by your child doesn't always feel good. Sometimes it tears you apart. You weigh the options, you listen to your instincts, and you still walk away wondering if you've just traded one kind of pain for another. And even when the results prove you right, even when progress shows up on the page, the questions never fully leave. That's the hidden weight parents carry, the tension between what you know has to be done and what your child wishes could stay the same.

I'd love to believe we won't have to make sacrifices like this again, but I know better. This is the reality of raising a child in a world that wasn't built with her in mind. Every season brings new obstacles, and with them, new choices that test our resolve. We'll keep making those choices, because she deserves a life without barriers holding her back. But I won't pretend it doesn't take something from us too.

The truth is, advocating for your child can be relentless. It asks you to stay steady when you're exhausted, to hold your ground when it'd be easier to let go, to build a path forward when no one else is offering one. It's not glamorous work, and it rarely gets celebrated, but it matters. And for as long as I'm here, I'll keep doing it. I'll keep showing up, even when it breaks my heart, because that's the promise I made the day she was born.

This past year changed us in ways we could see every single day. We watched Ella grow, step by step, and we felt ourselves growing alongside her. There was no clear roadmap, so we focused on what was in front of us. We stayed present, moved with patience, and learned to trust the small steps as much as the big ones. Little by little, a foundation began to form, built from the people who showed up for her, from the conversations that shaped our choices, and from a shared belief that something better was possible.

Growth like this doesn't happen by accident though. It comes from trust that's earned, encouragement that's steady, and patience that never runs out. It comes from people who see potential and choose to nurture it each day. This past year has shown us how the right environment can open new doors, not only for learning, but for how a person sees themselves. For Ella, it's meant stepping into each day with a stronger sense of who she is and what she can do. For us, it's meant knowing she's in a place where her future can continue to take root and grow.

You should see how each morning now begins. When Ms. Roxie arrives, Ella runs to greet her and wraps her in a big, huge hug. It's joy, trust, and belonging gathered into a single embrace. In time, that simple act has become the starting point for her best learning, a daily reminder that she's safe, valued, and free to explore. From that place, her confidence has grown, and so has her readiness to reach for what's possible.

This may not be the exact high school we'd always imagined for her, but it has become the one Ella needed most. Here, she's rediscovered her spark, deepened her joy, and has begun to learn on her own terms.

This is where we've built something new that will serve as the foundation for her journey forward. And for us, that makes it everything.

CHAPTER 9
THE PROPER CADENCE

In telling Ella's story, it's impossible not to tell her sister's, because if there's anyone I know who's future has astonishing potential, it's our Cadence, most affectionately known as Cady. Her ability to take on this world over the last thirteen years has been remarkable, and as someone who's seen her develop first hand, I have to say I'm a bit jealous.

Cady's coming of age is at odds with my own upbringing, because hers is a wide-open exploration of the world, and I'm doing everything I can to ensure she's able to pursue her passions. I never knew how curious I was about the world and didn't realize how far I'd go to experience life and living until much later in life. But, in Cady, I already see a much more developed sensibility and awareness of the infinite paths life has to offer. I can only imagine the journeys she'll eventually be chasing, and all the winding roads she'll travel, all in the name of creating her own beautiful life.

Of course, one would wonder at this point whether having a sister with Down syndrome will shape or constrain that path. Will she feel the need to stay close? Will she transition soon to making significant decisions on behalf of her sister? Does that mean she'll have to create a life that she may not envision for herself?

While these and similar questions are completely valid and logical, they're also big, nuanced, and layered questions that I don't have answers for at the moment. But I also don't think it's my place to come up with these answers, because they're fundamentally her decisions. Still, I have no doubt many of these thoughts have already started percolating through that beautiful mind of hers. And, I'm equally certain that in time, and as we all continue growing, she'll do right by herself and our family.

What I can say is that, as her parents, we'll forever try our best to afford her as liberating a life as possible, while being grateful for every ounce of her love and care. All along, everything we've built for Ella has, in some way, been built for both sisters, and it'll always remain this way. In fact, every step we've taken as a family, every celebration, every monumental achievement, has unfolded with both of them as the center piece. And though they won't be walking the same path or looking for the same bridges to cross, creating a more inclusive and empathetic world where more doors are opened rather than closed, can only benefit Cady and the world around her. This, unto itself, is the beauty of working on behalf of those with special needs.

Breakaway

You know, we talk about inclusion like it's some noble act, but I think we've been framing it wrong. This isn't about offering kindness to a small group of students. It's about building a world where no one's potential is left to the side.

When we make space for Ella, we're making space for Cady too, and for everyone else who follows. Inclusion expands what's possible for all of us. Every time a school reimagines how to teach, or a workplace opens its doors, or a community decides that belonging is non-negotiable, the ripple stretches further than we can see. It lifts every student, every colleague, every neighbor who was waiting for permission to be more fully themselves.

That's why I see inclusion as more than a moral choice. It's the smartest investment we can make in each other. When we give students the chance to show what they can do, everybody wins. The classroom gets richer, the workplace grows stronger, the community becomes more resilient. It's not charity and it's not sacrifice. It's about designing a world that doesn't waste talent or possibility, a world that brings hidden brilliance into view.

I've come to believe the measure of any society isn't found in how it treats its strongest, but in how it welcomes those who were never expected to succeed. Inclusion is the truest form of progress because it allows all of us to rise together. And when that happens, the lives of students like Ella and Cady aren't just supported, they're celebrated. The future they inherit becomes bigger than any dream we dared to imagine alone.

Much of what you've read so far has been seen through Ella's eyes, and that makes sense because her journey has been the thread holding these chapters together. But right alongside it runs another story, much more subtle in some ways, yet just as defining. It belongs to the younger sister who's been alongside us, chasing every mile, every new day, and every dream we've carried as a family. So it stands to reason that to truly understand Ella's story, you have to know Cady's too, because while their paths are different, they've always been intertwined.

From the very beginning, Cady has brought strength and joy to our family. I can still picture her in the high chair beside me, legs swinging above the floor, a colorful bib around her neck as she shared countless meals with her sister. Those early days were full of small rituals like that, breakfast on the countertop, afternoon naps, and evenings spent watching television on the living room floor. These were the moments that imbued her into our family's rhythm. As she grew up, that same ease transcended into the world around us. She moved naturally into new environments, following along as we introduced both of them to different activities. Sometimes she would join in without hesitation, other times she would stand back, watching closely until she understood the rhythm of the place, then finding her own way into it as though she'd been there all along.

Amazingly enough, those moments outside the home have always found their way back into the life we share within it. At home, where she's most at ease, Cady moves through the space with a natural rhythm, never seeking the spotlight yet somehow drawing it in. She might settle into her room with a book or her laptop, pause in the kitchen to have the freshly cut fruit that's always waiting on the counter, or wander into the backyard with Jack at her side, our faithful Labrador following her, knowing she's the keeper of his best life. Regardless of how she spends her time though, she brings a presence that warms the house and softens the edges of even the longest days.

Through it all, she's learned what perseverance looks like, not from books or speeches, but from seeing it lived out in front of her. She's watched her sister take on challenges that others doubted she could meet, seen the strain in her face and the slump of her shoulders when the work feels defeating, and felt the validation that follows a great achievement. These moments were never staged as lessons for her, but they became lessons all the same. One by one, they've shaped the way she sees the world and her place in it, leaving her with an understanding that real progress is built between the lines, during long stretches of hard work when no one's watching.

Over the years, their bond has been shaped as much by the everyday as by the extraordinary. The big moments always stand out, but it's the small, uninteresting ones that've built the relationship between them. Being Ella's younger sister was never something Cady had to pause and consider in those early years. They played, argued, and laughed like any sisters, moving through their days without thinking about what made them different. They learned side by side, shared the same spaces, and treated the world as something to discover together, one adventure at a time. Over the years though, Cady's begun to understand more of what it means for Ella to have Down syndrome. She notices the ways her sister learns at a different pace, the moments when patience really matters, and the times when a few words of encouragement can change everything.

At thirteen, she's shaping her own life, learning how to be there for her sister while also making space for herself. Some days she drifts into her own world, recharging on her own terms. Other days she leans all the way in, joining Ella in the gym or curling up in the family room to watch a show they both love. And even if she doesn't often say it, I know she carries a deep awareness of her sister's journey and a pride in how far Ella's come.

Cady's been part of Ella's story from the very beginning, shaping her in ways no school or therapy session could. She's been the sister who shows up, the one who knows when to push and when to step back, and the steady presence who's seen every win, setback, and in-between moment. Growing up together has taught them both patience, empathy, and the compromise that comes from sharing so much of life side by side.

It's in the way Ella lights up when she sees her sister after a week of camp. It's in the small, everyday things too, like helping each other in the gym, laughing over the same joke, or just sitting together in comfortable silence. At the end of the day, if you really want to understand who Ella is, and what we hope for her future, you have to account for the part Cady's played all along, because she's been right there, helping to build the road her sister's walking.

Cadence, as she's officially named, came into the world three years after Ella. She arrived when so much of our attention was already on her sister's needs, yet she seemed to find her place as if it'd been waiting for her all along. From the start, she carried herself with a kind of poise that made her seem older than her years, as if she already understood that life had its own rhythm and that she could move through it as she pleased.

From the start, she had a way of making the smallest moments feel important. There was an ease about her that drew you in, the kind that made you want to watch just a little longer, to take in who she was becoming even in the most ordinary parts of the day. Now in eighth grade, she negotiates the world in a way that draws people in before they even realize it.

Someone meeting her for the first time might think she's simply reserved, letting the conversation unfold around her while others take the lead. But if you pay attention, you see how fully present she is. Her eyes move from face to face, catching the tone of a voice, the shift of a gesture, the weight of a pause. She listens with intention, gathering the small details of a moment before choosing how and when to step in.

To me, it's quite extraordinary how she doesn't compete for space in a room, yet somehow fills it with a presence that brings a sense of balance. People seem to stand a little differently around her, as if her calm invites them to settle too. And, there's a steadiness in the way she carries herself, a strength in her posture, as though she knows exactly who she is and feels no need to prove it. It's a very admirable character trait really, the kind that comes from knowing your own abilities and trusting them. So, it's no surprise that both younger children and her peers are drawn to her, sensing that same ease and calmness.

It's not just her presence that stands out, but the way her mind works, so much so that her creativity was impossible to miss. Though I may be biased as her father, her paintings and drawings have always felt beyond her years, each one showing a level of detail and imagination that I've always considered extraordinary.

What I really love is how she's always had a way of making things her own. Give her a blank page, a volleyball, or a free afternoon, and she'll turn it into something entirely hers. She doesn't follow someone else's path simply because it's easier. Instead, she searches for what inspires her, what sparks her curiosity, and then she commits to it fully. That search has carried her through many worlds, but in each place, she brings the same focus and drive, as if the act of doing something well matters every bit as much as the outcome.

These days, volleyball has become her anchor, the place she returns to no matter what else is happening in her life. You can see the joy it gives her in the way she settles into its rhythm, in the sound of the ball meeting her hands, in the quick exchange of glances with a teammate, in the shared breath before a serve.

At home, there's almost always a volleyball in her hands. I see her in the backyard, sometimes under the afternoon sun, other times under the porch light, practicing her serves and passes against a net, likely imagining herself in the middle of a big game. That same focus follows her into her creative life. She has a natural gift with the arts, a knack for shaping ideas into life that's often astonishing.

Breakaway

When you're raising two kids together, you start to see how much they shape each other without even trying. It's not just the big stuff like birthdays or family trips. It's in the little things most people would never notice. The way one watches the other, the way they pick up each other's habits without thinking about it. Cady has had a front row seat to Ella's life, and whether she realizes it or not, it's been teaching her about perseverance, patience, and compassion in a way no book ever could. That's the thing about siblings. You never know which moments will stick, but they're always there, shaping who you become.

Cady's learned what resilience looks like not because we sat her down and explained it, but because she's watched her sister live it. She's seen Ella stumble and try again. She's seen her fight through frustration, celebrate victories that others might dismiss, and keep moving when the road was anything but smooth. Those lessons don't disappear. They seep into you quietly, shaping the way you see yourself and the way you see the world.

And it works both ways. Ella has grown because Cady has been there too, not just as a playmate or a companion, but as someone who sees her without judgment. She's the sister who laughs at her jokes, shares her routines, and gives her the dignity of being seen as more than a diagnosis. That's no small thing. It's a lifeline. Because every student with disabilities deserves someone who reminds them they're not defined by what others assume, but by who they are in the eyes of those who love them most.

As parents, we hope to give both of them everything they need, but the truth is, siblings end up teaching each other in ways we never could. They're the ones who share the quiet hours, the unremarkable days, the space where real life unfolds. And those ordinary moments, repeated over years, do more to shape character than any grand speech ever could.

That's what makes me believe Cady's path, whatever she chooses, will always be grounded in something rare. She's seen what it means to stand beside someone who's underestimated. She's learned what it looks like when progress takes longer than expected. And she's been part of a home where love had to be intentional, where patience had to be practiced, and where belonging was never negotiable. Those lessons will travel with her wherever she goes.

Still, there's one memory that has never faded for me, one that I return to again and again when I think about who Cady is and how I want her to carry herself in the world. Most mornings, back when she was seven or so, she would lead me to our favorite spot at school, a place where a single tree has been rooted since the seventies when the school was built. She would take a big step onto the ledge that surrounded the trunk, balancing herself before turning to me. I would crouch down, adjust the straps of her pink backpack so they sat comfortably against her shoulders, smooth her hair, and kiss her cheeks. She would smile, wave, and say, "Bye, Daddy," before walking into the stream of students.

Some mornings I lingered, watching her until she disappeared around the corner. Other days I left quickly, already looking forward to the moment I would see her again in the afternoon. It was such a small ritual, something that countless parents all over the world do every day, but for me it carried a significance I could never fully explain. Maybe it was the way she faced each day even at that age, steady, ready, and quietly radiant. Or, maybe it was my own awe at the gift the universe had given me in her.

I think about that morning ritual now, and I see how it was never just about walking little Cady to school. It was about the way she moves through the world. She's cautious yet confident, observant yet fully engaged. It was about the way she holds her place in this family, always connected to her sister, yet carving out her own life. I find it remarkable how she's able to navigate these paradoxes so seamlessly.

The truth is, my work for Ella has always been for Cady too. What I want for one, I want for both. Opportunity, belonging, and a future they can define on their own terms. When I think about the chapters that have come before, the school meetings, the moments of joy and defiance, the steps forward and the steps back, I see that Cady has been in the frame all along. She's been learning what it means to fight for something and has come to understand that change is slow, that hard things are worth doing, and that there is no substitute for showing up every day and doing the work.

This book has never been about a single person. It's about all the people who walk alongside one another to create a more inclusive world, and the ones who will eventually inherit the bridges we're building. That includes Cady. In fact, especially Cady.

CHAPTER 10
READY ALL ALONG

We think we know what it means to open a door. It feels simple enough most days, like the kind of gesture that lingers somewhere between habit and kindness. You hold a door open, step aside, and give someone the privilege of stepping in front of you. You're headed in the same direction for the most part, so there's mutual acknowledgement, maybe a smile or a nod, and you move on with the rest of your day.

But I've learned over time that opening a door isn't just about courtesy. Some doors, both literal and figurative, offer passage into a space completely different from the one you're in. Matter of fact, a door held open can change the entire story for the person who steps through. In these instances, what once felt unreachable can become the beginning of something entirely new. And, for anyone who's watched a life unfold on the other side, the gesture is anything but small.

Unfortunately, the doors that matter most are rarely the obvious ones. More often than not, they're the ones we're told not to expect, the ones that hide in the background until someone points them out. Sometimes we're told they were sealed long ago, never meant for us, and especially not for the ones we love. Those discouraging messages inherently leave marks, and over time they shape what we believe is possible, teaching us to stop searching for openings that others insist are not there.

That's what it often feels like when you're raising a child with Down syndrome. For sixteen years with Ella, we've been told, sometimes outright and sometimes in subtle ways, to lower our gaze, to accept limits before they've been tested, and to stop looking for possibilities that others have already decided don't exist. And yet every part of me knows those assumptions don't come close to reflecting the amount of potential she truly has.

What I've learned is that doors can shift, even when they seem permanently closed. It never happens all at once though. Instead, a parent stays at the table, asks the questions that matter, and shows up again when the conversation could have ended. Notes are sent, meetings continue, and a path begins to gradually form where nothing had existed. From the outside these parents might seem stubborn, maybe even naive and unwilling to accept reality. But up close, their actions are purely love in the form of persistence, guided by possibility, and the conviction that the world can always make room for one more step, one more chance, one more child.

I've spent years holding on to the hope that Ella will be given her chance. Every conversation late into the night, every meeting that ended without answers, every hope that stretched further than reason allowed has been tied to that vision. I imagine her stepping into a place that wasn't built with her in mind and by simply being there, making it her own.

In my mind I can already see it. She takes her seat in a classroom, joins the discussion, and begins the work of learning. She walks across campus as though it belongs to her. She blends into the flow of daily life, not as a visitor or an exception, but as a student in full. It's in those seemingly ordinary moments that the extraordinary shows itself, when what once seemed impossible begins to look exactly how it should've looked all along.

The truth is Ella hasn't reached that point yet, though I absolutely believe she will. What matters is that we keep moving forward, with each day building on the last. Every conversation, every effort, every piece of the path we've stitched together has always kept her in focus. And when her moment does come, I'll remind her of what has always been true. That the joy and determination she brings has never needed permission to matter. That the world is only now beginning to see what we've known all along.

Breakaway

I know it isn't always realistic to expect the world to accommodate every student with intellectual disabilities or to assume they'll always be supported and welcomed. While that may be true, it doesn't lessen our responsibility to be the first ones to believe in a better tomorrow for them. The truth is, if families like ours don't believe first, no one else will.

Belief is where real change begins, but belief alone isn't enough. It takes persistence. It takes walking into rooms where you're outnumbered and still refusing to give up. It takes asking questions that make people uncomfortable, insisting on answers that aren't easy, and showing up again when the system hopes you'll give up. This is what it means to widen the room. It's the daily work that tests your patience, your strength, and sometimes even your faith.

And here's the truth most people never see. Behind every win there are dozens of setbacks. Behind every open door there are nights of doubt and mornings where you wonder if it's worth it. Too often, society wants to celebrate the visible triumph without acknowledging the exhausting road that led there. We applaud the moment a student with disabilities walks across a stage, but we rarely ask about the years of advocacy, the battles fought in silence, the tears shed in parking lots after another meeting that went nowhere.

That's why I believe inclusion has to stop being seen as an act of kindness and start being understood as a collective responsibility. This isn't about doing favors. It's about building a society that doesn't waste human potential, a society that refuses to throw away the brilliance that sits quietly in classrooms, waiting to be seen.

And if the world hasn't made enough room yet, then it's on us to widen it. Not just for our own children, but for every student who deserves to step through a door and find more than tolerance. They deserve belonging. They deserve opportunity. They deserve a future that doesn't hinge on someone else's permission.

As I've walked this path, I've learned Ella's story isn't hers alone. Again and again I've heard the same truth echoed by other families. Parents described the moment they first saw their son or daughter walking across campus and how liberating that felt. Students spoke about the freedom of choosing their own classes, finding friends, and being recognized for who they were. Faculty members told me about the joy of watching possibility take shape, of seeing expectations rise and then be met. However it was told, every story carried the same message. The journey began when someone with privilege chose to open a door wide enough for a student to walk through.

Hearing those stories gave me hope, but they also sharpened the ache of not yet knowing what that would feel like for Ella. I could describe it in conversations, even map out what I thought it could become, but it was still only imagined. I longed for the moment when she might walk through her own door, when possibility would shift from theory to lived experience.

That began to change one December weekend when we visited an inclusive postsecondary program for the first time.

We arrived curious, unsure of what we might find, but eager for even a glimpse of what college life could mean for students like Ella. The program director welcomed us with warmth and took us on a walk through campus, speaking with the kind of clarity that comes only from lived experience. As both a director and a mother, she shared her own story, weaving together the professional and the personal in a way that made every word carry weight. She talked about students who had found their voice on campus, about the subtle but undeniable ways their presence shifted the rhythm of classrooms, and about how inclusion was slowly becoming part of daily life.

Later, over coffee, we continued the conversation. We asked question after question about how the program came to be, how it was sustained, and what it took to keep every student not only learning but also happy and safe. She answered with honesty, never hiding the challenges but always grounding them in possibility. Before we left, she told us about a student showcase scheduled for the next morning and encouraged us to return, to see the program not just through her eyes but through the work and presence of the students themselves.

So the next day, which happened to be a Saturday, we came back. By then most of the campus was empty, students already gone for winter break, and it felt as though the life of the place had gathered indoors. We found our way to the hall where the showcase was being held and stepped carefully into the room, trying not to intrude on families who clearly belonged there. At first, we stayed off to the side, taking it all in. But the longer we watched, the more our hesitation gave way. The space was alive. Tables stretched across the room, each one filled with projects shaped by effort and imagination. Students stood beside their work, explaining with pride what they'd created. Their words carried not only knowledge but ownership. Faculty and staff moved through the crowd with ease, their presence steady and encouraging, their voices filled with conviction that made you stop and listen.

In that room, the pieces I had only imagined began to take shape in real time. It was no longer an idea or a distant possibility. It was happening in front of us, lived out by students who had been given the chance to belong. They weren't framed as exceptions, nor were they asked to prove their worth. They were simply present, sharing themselves as learners, creators, and peers. And as I watched, I realized that this was not just their story but a glimpse of what Ella's could become. It was proof that the door we had been knocking on for so long could indeed open, and that on the other side was not a dream but a future already being lived.

Ella was there that day with her sister by her side. We moved slowly through the rows, stopping at tables, listening as students explained their projects, smiling at their pride, and nodding at their confidence. I was already struck by the life in the room, the laughter, the easy conversations, the way students leaned forward as if their work carried weight, because it did. The space felt charged with possibility, and when I glanced at my wife, I caught the same expression in her eyes. It was recognition, the shared sense that we had finally arrived at what we'd been hoping to see.

Even so, I felt a strange distance standing there. Years earlier I'd been an undergraduate on that same campus, walking those sidewalks with a backpack on my shoulders and a head full of ambitions that now seem small compared to what unfolded in life. Back then, the future was something abstract, open-ended. I never could have imagined returning one day, as a father searching for signs of my daughter's future.

Sometimes I think about what that younger version of me would've seen if he'd caught even a glimpse of this moment. He wouldn't have grasped the love, the responsibility, or the mix of fear and joy that lay ahead. At first he might have been confused, maybe even doubtful. But if he'd stayed long enough, he would've seen it for what it was: a life that would ask more of him than he thought he could give, and give back more than he ever imagined.

I remember looking around, taking in the hum of voices and the pride that seemed to fill the room, and wondering how Ella was seeing it all through her own eyes. Then near one of the displays she tugged at me and spoke words that rose above all the background chatter. They've stayed with me ever since.

She waited until I looked at her, and with steady certainty she said, "Daddy, that girl has Downs too." Her eyes were fixed on the students in front of us, her voice clear and sure. It wasn't a question. It wasn't whispered. It was a statement, plain and true. She wasn't just observing what she saw. She was locating herself in the world.

I'd always believed this moment would come, though I never knew when or how. That belief carried me through appointments, meetings, and years of conversations about her future. Still, hearing her claim it for herself was something different. It was no longer my vision projected forward. It was her voice, her truth, spoken in real time. It landed with a force that caught me off guard, reminding me that all the years of steady faith had led to this. Ella was seeing herself, fully and without hesitation, in a space that once seemed unreachable.

Breakaway

It's easy for people to underestimate how much it means to see yourself in someone else's story. For families like ours, those moments are rare, and when they do come, they arrive with the kind of force that leaves a mark. Because the truth is, most of the world is still organized around telling students like Ella what they can't do, where they don't belong, and why their futures must be smaller than everyone else's.

That's why spaces like this matter. They prove that possibility isn't theoretical, it's lived. They show that when we open doors wide enough, students walk through and remind us of their capacity, their brilliance, their right to belong. But these spaces don't just appear on their own. They're built by people who are willing to resist what's easy, to question what's been normalized, and to invest in a vision most others dismiss too quickly.

For me, standing in that showcase was a reminder of what's at stake. We aren't fighting for charity, or for pity, or for someone else's version of kindness. We're fighting for equity, for dignity, for the chance every student deserves to be recognized as capable. And if we're honest, it shouldn't take this much effort to prove what should have been obvious all along.

Ella's words that morning cut through all of it. They weren't dressed up or softened. They were simple and true. And in that clarity was the reminder of why we keep showing up, why we keep knocking on doors until they open, why we can't afford to let silence or fatigue set the pace. Because every student deserves the chance to stand in their own light, to say "this is who I am," and to know the world is ready to receive them.

That morning was never just a student showcase. It was a glimpse of the world as it could be. A world where students with intellectual disabilities aren't pushed to the margins but stand at the center of their own stories. A world where possibility isn't rationed, where doors aren't locked, where the worth of a life isn't decided by what others call realistic.

And in Ella's voice, steady and certain, I heard that future already speaking. It told me that belonging isn't abstract. It's real, it's urgent, and it begins the moment we choose to believe in it. It told me that all the years of persistence, all the questions and the waiting and the doubt, had been leading us here. And it reminded me that hope is not fragile. Hope grows stronger when it's spoken aloud, when it's claimed without hesitation, when it's lived in the open for everyone to see.

That morning, Ella wasn't just seeing herself in someone else's story. She was stepping into her own. And that is where every new chapter begins.

CHAPTER 11
THIS IS THE WORK

The truth I felt from Ella's words didn't fade as the morning went on. It only grew clearer the longer we stayed in that room. What I witnessed through her eyes, that sense of recognition and belonging, was alive in the space around us. The students weren't simply participating. They were flourishing. Their projects carried curiosity shaped by guidance, and intellect expressed with confidence. In that moment, it was clear this was more than a showcase. It was a glimpse of what education can become when students are allowed to stand fully in their own light.

Families stood nearby, some holding back tears as they watched their sons and daughters step into roles that had always been waiting for them. Faculty members leaned in with genuine admiration for what these students had created. The energy in the room was unmistakable. It wasn't staged or forced, but rather lived and real. And as I stood there, I knew we weren't just witnessing a moment of success. We were seeing a vision of what's possible when education chooses to honor every student's potential.

What struck me most that day was not only what I saw in Ella, but what I recognized in every parent in that room. Their faces held the same blend of awe and relief, as if a future they'd only hoped for was now unfolding in front of them. I thought about the many families I'd met over the years, through conversations, through support groups, through chance encounters in waiting rooms and hallways. If there's one thread that runs through nearly every conversation, it's fear. Fear of what will happen when we're no longer here to advocate. Fear that our children will be cherished at home, but overlooked in the world because of unrecognized potential. That fear is real and it follows us everywhere.

But when we find ourselves in spaces where our children are seen, even for a moment, that fear loosens its grip. Recognition begins to take the place of doubt, and what felt impossible suddenly feels within reach. Moments like that don't just ease our worries, they point us forward. They remind us what education can be when it's rooted in possibility. Most importantly, they show us that inclusion isn't simply a moral obligation we're all held to. True inclusion is in the work itself, the real test of whether our values show up in practice and not just in words.

That day was a glimpse of a future already unfolding, and a visible call to action. If we want more of these moments to move from rare to routine, then we ought to build differently. We ought to move beyond single programs and courageous families, and instead shape institutions that are ready, sustainable, and committed to equity at their core. This is the work ahead.

At the heart of it all is belief. I saw it in Ella that morning, in the way she recognized herself in the projects around her and in the way her confidence grew because others reflected that belief back to her. Moments like that show us what's possible, but they don't last without conviction. Systems don't change and programs don't endure unless belief is at their core. More than resources, more than planning, more than structure, belief is what creates the commitment to futures written on their own terms.

When I look back, I realize that so many of Ella's most important moments began with someone choosing to believe. A doctor who looked beyond a diagnosis. A teacher who spoke to her as a student first. A peer who waved her over instead of walking past. Each gesture was small on its own, yet together they created a rhythm that shaped how she saw herself and how we began to see what was possible for her.

The showcase was one of those moments, but at the same time, it also embodied something larger and more universal. The fact that an entire community had chosen to be there together made that room feel different. That's why Ella recognized herself there, and that revelation is ultimately what drew me into this work. If ever there was an origin story to explain the reinvention of my life and career, it'd be traced directly back to the rainy morning. I made a decision that day that changed the entire trajectory of our family's future, and I haven't looked back since.

Along the way, I've met many leaders across the country, some with vast resources, others with almost none. Not surprisingly, what I remember most isn't their polished presentations or slide decks, but their honesty and authenticity. Many have told me the same thing, that they've seen the goodness in people when they're given the chance to support a student with an intellectual disability. They're right and it's so true. When given the chance, classmates rise. Professors learn and expand their perspectives. Staff rediscover why they entered education in the first place. And students, the very ones underestimated, become the proof of what inclusion was always meant to look like. They remind us that education shouldn't be about sorting or excluding, but about opening doors wide enough for every learner to find their place.

I also know now that when inclusion is real, you can feel it. It's not just a student sitting in the back of a classroom. It's the way a peer leans over to share notes, or the way a professor lights up when a question shifts the conversation, or the way a staff member pauses to realize that their role is bigger than paperwork, that they're helping someone's future take root. These aren't grand gestures, but together they change the very essence of a room.

Perhaps it was happening unconsciously, but Ella's been showing me this since the beginning. Every time she walks into a space, she brings the possibility of connection. When she waves at a classmate, she's offering recognition. When she sings from the passenger seat of the car, she's filling the air with her presence. None of it is manufactured, and yet each moment reveals something essential about inclusion. Belonging isn't created by systems or granted by permission. It's already within us, waiting to be recognized.

What Ella reveals so effortlessly is often the very thing the world overlooks. Her openness, her connection, her joy are reminders of what inclusion can be. Yet too often, limits are placed on her that have nothing to do with who she is. They grow out of fear, misunderstanding, or a failure of imagination. But when those limits fall away and belief takes their place, she shines in ways that tell the truth about who we might all become if we dared to see one another fully.

That's why I couldn't just be a parent who waits on the sidelines, hoping the system would change on its own. Ella's life made the gaps impossible to ignore, and her way of showing what was possible made it impossible to accept them as permanent. What began as a father's determination grew into a responsibility to build what was missing, to shape the kind of spaces where she and others like her could see themselves reflected.

That work didn't start in boardrooms or classrooms though. It started in the thoughtful and pragmatic spaces of our own home. Most of what I've tried to build began small, at our kitchen table after long days at school, in the worrisome tone of late-night conversations about what could be better. To a large extent, it was both fear and hope that kept us going. Fear is what kept me awake in the dead of night, annoyingly whispering all the ways the world might fail my daughter. But hope is what I woke up to each morning, always reminding me that more is possible. Rather than treating them as opposites, I've learned to hold both at once, letting their tension guide my work and return me to what matters most.

Breakaway

If you take nothing else from this chapter, let it be this. Belief is where it begins. Not resources, not approval, not permission. Just belief.

But belief isn't passive. It's not sitting back and hoping things work out. It's the decision to show up again and again, even when the room feels cold or the answers don't come. It's the refusal to let someone else's lowered expectations define what's possible for your student. It's asking the harder question, writing the extra email, sitting through one more meeting, because you know what's at stake.

Belief is where everything that matters in education has ever started. A teacher who believed a student could learn before the data showed it. A peer who believed inclusion could be more than a word on a poster. A parent who believed their child's future was worth fighting for, even when the world told them to stop asking. Every program that exists, every door that has opened, began with someone willing to believe first.

And here's the truth. Belief costs nothing, but it changes everything. You don't need a budget line to offer it. You don't need a committee to approve it. You just need the courage to see what's in front of you and to act as if it matters. Because it does.

If you believe in a student, you don't just change their outlook. You change the room around them. You shift the way others see them, the way the system responds, the way possibility takes root. Belief creates momentum, and momentum creates change. And that's how new futures begin.

What I know now is that this work isn't only about Ella. It's about every student who's been underestimated, every parent who's lived with both fear and hope, every educator who's wondered if belief might be enough. The story doesn't end in a single classroom or even in a single family. If inclusion is to last, belief has to move from moments into structures, from conversations into frameworks, from individual conviction into the very design of our institutions. That's where the work ahead begins.

I turned to research not to replace what I had learned as a father, but to deepen it. I wanted to listen to other families, to students themselves, to faculty and administrators who were building programs in real time. I wanted to know what was working, what held promise, and what still stood in the way.

What I found didn't live only in transcripts or reports. It lived in the questions parents whisper late at night and in the hopes that rise each morning with their children. It lived in the voices of students daring to imagine more for themselves and in the courage of educators willing to believe alongside them. Research gave me language, and more so, it revealed a vision of what is possible when belief expands beyond individuals. It showed me how belief can become collective, how it can take root in systems and endure. That understanding became the foundation for my doctoral work, and it's to those insightful findings and recommendations that I now turn.

CHAPTER 12
COLLECTIVELY BECOMING

It's easy to believe that students with intellectual disabilities are absent from college because they somehow chose not to be there, that perhaps they lacked the motivation, the academic preparation, or the maturity to handle the responsibility. It's even easier to assume that college simply wasn't the right fit, and that in some unspoken way they must have known this themselves. Yet that isn't the truth. It's only the version of the story that's been repeated so often, across so many years, that we stopped questioning it.

The truth rests not in individual shortcomings but in the absence of expectation. These students were never imagined as part of the design. There was no seat saved for them in the lecture hall, no counselor prepared to guide them through applications, no syllabus written with their name in mind. The entire scaffolding of higher education, from its policies to its definitions of success, was built with a particular kind of student at the center, and everyone else, especially those with intellectual disabilities, was left on the margins before the door even opened.

From an academic standpoint, this absence is striking. The World Health Organization defines intellectual disability as a condition that is characterized by significant limitations in both intellectual functioning and adaptive behavior. That definition does not in itself exclude the possibility of higher education. If anything, it underscores the importance of appropriate support and structure, not the absence of potential. Still, students with intellectual disabilities remain among the most underrepresented groups in all of higher education. Data from the National Center for Education Statistics shows that students with disabilities overall enroll in and complete college at significantly lower rates than their nondisabled peers. For students with intellectual disabilities, the gap is even greater, with national studies indicating that only a small fraction access postsecondary opportunities, despite the expansion of inclusive programs in recent years.

That outcome isn't accidental. It's the result of design. Access to college has long been tied to academic indicators such as standardized tests, grade point averages, admissions essays, and letters of recommendation. These measures reflect far more about a student's access to resources and accommodations than about their actual potential to succeed. And beneath these structural barriers lies another obstacle, one less visible yet deeply entrenched: belief, or rather the lack of it.

A system built on traditional notions of meritocracy often carries assumptions about who is capable of success and who is not. In this way, the bar itself becomes the gate, and the gate becomes the culture, until exclusion is so normalized that it blends into the background.

That's what happened to Ella. By the time she reached high school, her exclusion had already been scripted. Not by malicious intent, not by individual neglect, but by a structure that consistently delivered the same result. She was funneled into course offerings that didn't count toward a diploma, her transition plan emphasized life skills without ever mentioning college, and her teachers, though compassionate, had never thought much about supporting a student with Down syndrome in pursuing higher education. This wasn't a failure at the individual level. It was the system doing exactly what it had been built to do.

That absence of belief became the foundation for everything that followed. It shaped policy, and policy shaped practice, until repetition itself created culture. That culture wrapped itself in the language of access and equity but rarely stopped to notice who was missing from the room. And unless someone intervened, unless someone chose to challenge the assumptions and rewrite the plan, Ella, like so many others, would vanish from the story of higher education before her first chapter had even begun.

But this moment is different. We're no longer left with only anecdotes or vague inspiration. We have research. We have evidence. We have programs across the country that show when students with intellectual disabilities are given pathways, they take them. When they're supported with mentoring, inclusive coursework, and genuine peer engagement, they flourish. And when we measure their success not by conformity but by growth, by employment, independence, and self advocacy, the outcomes speak with clarity.

The Higher Education Opportunity Act of 2008 recognized this truth when it opened the door to Comprehensive Transition and Postsecondary programs. TPSID grants gave institutions the resources to begin building inclusive models, and those programs became a signal of what was possible. Yet they were never meant to be the finish line. They were the starting point for a movement still too rare, too fragile, and too dependent on a handful of determined families and visionary leaders.

And this is where my own journey runs parallel. I've been on this path since the day Ella arrived, long before I ever considered myself a researcher. The questions began then, wondering about what her future would hold and how the world would respond to her presence. Over the years, those questions grew alongside her, and they shaped the choices we made as a family, the battles we fought in classrooms, and the hopes we carried through every transition. Enrolling in a doctoral program wasn't the beginning of this work, it was simply the moment I chose to give form and discipline to what I had already been living.

As a student, I spent evenings and weekends immersed in classes, often staring into a screen after the house had gone still, sometimes exchanging ideas with peers who were wrestling with their own questions about leadership and change. I read constantly, I wrote relentlessly, and little by little I learned the cadence of research. The program gave me language and structure, but the heart of the work had always been Ella. The academic process refined my perspective and strengthened my resolve, teaching me to hold details with care and patterns with precision, but the urgency of the work was never abstract. It was the life unfolding in front of me.

Through that process, I began to recognize that the voices I was hearing carried more than individual stories. They carried directions. Some pointed toward belonging, reminding us that education is never just about content but about community. Others pointed toward infrastructure, showing that programs cannot survive on passion alone but must be supported by systems designed to endure. Still others pointed toward resources and sustainability, a reminder that without investment even the most inspiring ideas eventually falter. And some pointed toward belief itself, the conviction that students with intellectual disabilities not only deserve to be in higher education but bring something essential to their lives.

Together, these directions formed a constellation, an orientation I could no longer ignore. They created a way of seeing higher education differently, not through abstractions but through the bearings of students and families who had too often been left outside the design.

What follows in this chapter isn't a list of conclusions. It's the weaving of those directions into findings that matter. They aren't only my interpretations but the shared wisdom of students, families, and educators who offered their voices and, in doing so, became both compass and map for the work ahead.

Belonging

Every story I heard, whether from students, parents, or program staff, circled back to one truth: belonging is not an extra, it is the foundation. Academic growth, social confidence, even the courage to pursue independence all begin with the assurance that you are seen, valued, and included. Without belonging, every other goal feels fragile. With it, doors open.

Students described the moments when they felt woven into the life of a campus, not as guests but as peers. A passing hello on the quad, an invitation to sit at a crowded lunch table, a shared laugh during a late study session all mattered because they signaled acceptance. Families spoke about the transformation they witnessed when their sons and daughters were recognized not for what they lacked, but for who they were. Faculty noted that when inclusion was authentic, students with intellectual disabilities didn't just benefit from the classroom, they reshaped it. Their presence reframed discussions, offered perspectives others hadn't considered, and deepened the sense of community that education at its best should create.

For students who had spent years being tracked into separate spaces or reminded that they didn't fully belong, entering college carried a weight beyond academics. A syllabus with their name on it, a student ID card, or the chance to join a club became more than tokens of access. They became evidence that the institution had made room for them, that higher education had begun to reimagine who its students could be.

Programs that succeeded in cultivating belonging did so intentionally. They built peer mentoring systems that paired students with classmates committed to inclusion. They encouraged participation in campus clubs and leadership opportunities, signaling that belonging extended beyond the classroom. They trained faculty to see inclusive practice not as a burden but as part of effective teaching. Each of these strategies created points of connection, moving students from the edges of campus life into its center.

Belonging, then, isn't sentimental. It is structural. It is the condition that makes everything else possible. When students with intellectual disabilities know they belong, they are more likely to persist, to take risks, to advocate for themselves, and to see college not as a temporary placement but as the space where their futures begin to take shape.

Infrastrucutre

If belonging is the foundation, infrastructure is the framework that holds it steady. Programs that lasted and grew were not built on goodwill alone. They were built on systems that supported the work in ways both visible and unseen. Without structure, even the most inspiring program often faded once a key leader retired, a grant expired, or a budget cycle shifted. With it, inclusion had the chance to take root.

Faculty and administrators often pointed to the hidden work required to make programs viable. Advising systems had to be adapted so that counselors could guide students with intellectual disabilities through course selection, campus services, and career planning. Disability resource offices had to be integrated into broader academic life rather than serving as isolated outposts. Financial aid systems needed adjustments so students in inclusive programs could access federal support.

Each of these details, while technical, determined whether students could participate fully or whether barriers would quietly push them out.

Programs that endured also recognized the importance of cross-campus collaboration. Success did not belong to one office or one visionary leader. It required academic departments, student affairs, disability services, financial aid, housing, and career centers to share responsibility. When inclusive education was embedded into the institution's fabric, it became less vulnerable to turnover and more resilient over time.

Families often saw this difference firsthand. In some programs, communication was clear, procedures were transparent, and support systems were easy to navigate. In others, the burden fell heavily on parents to patch gaps, chase down answers, and advocate for every detail. The contrast revealed a central truth: infrastructure either distributes responsibility across the institution or shifts it onto families who are already carrying so much.

Infrastructure, then, is not simply about efficiency. It is about sustainability. It is the framework that transforms inclusion from a fragile project into an enduring practice. Without it, programs remain vulnerable. With it, they become part of the institution's identity, offering students with intellectual disabilities not only access but the assurance that their place on campus is permanent, not provisional.

Resources and Sustainability

If infrastructure provides the framework, resources are the lifeblood that allows programs to endure. Again and again, participants pointed to the reality that no matter how inspired the vision, without funding and staffing the work could not last. Grants opened doors, often serving as the catalyst for new programs, but sustainability required something deeper: a commitment by institutions to invest in inclusion as part of their core mission rather than as a temporary project.

Administrators spoke candidly about the challenges. TPSID grants created opportunities, but when funding cycles ended, many programs faced hard choices. Those that persisted often did so because institutions found ways to braid funding streams, integrating federal aid, state support, philanthropy, and tuition revenue. This patchwork approach was rarely seamless, but it reflected the determination to keep the work alive.

Faculty and staff also highlighted the importance of human resources. Programs needed trained coordinators, peer mentors, and faculty development to sustain quality. Without dedicated staffing, the burden often fell on a few individuals whose passion carried the program but whose capacity was stretched thin. Families saw this too, noting the difference between programs that had consistent points of contact and those that relied on ad hoc arrangements.

What became clear across every account was that resources were not only financial. Sustainability also depended on time, leadership attention, and institutional will. Programs that thrived did so because leaders treated inclusion not as an add-on but as a long-term investment in the identity of the campus. In these places, the conversation shifted from "Can we afford this?" to "Can we afford not to?"

Resources and sustainability, then, are more than practical concerns. They are statements of priority. When institutions commit real support, they send a signal that students with intellectual disabilities are not a passing initiative but an enduring part of higher education's future.

Belief

Even with belonging, infrastructure, and resources, one more element remained at the center of every story I heard. It was not a policy or a funding mechanism. It was belief. Without it, even the strongest systems faltered. With it, possibilities expanded in ways that no blueprint alone could guarantee.

Belief showed itself in subtle but unmistakable ways. A faculty member deciding to treat a student with intellectual disabilities as a learner first, not as a label. A peer mentor inviting a classmate into a group project rather than assuming they had nothing to contribute. An advisor setting goals that stretched rather than diminished. Each of these actions carried weight, because each one challenged the assumption that had excluded these students for so long.

Families often spoke of belief as the difference between resignation and hope. For years they had been told, directly or indirectly, that college was out of reach. When someone within higher education finally said, "Yes, your student belongs here," it was more than encouragement. It was a rewriting of what was possible. Students themselves echoed this, describing how their confidence grew not only from what they achieved, but from the knowledge that others saw them as capable of achievement.

Programs that flourished were those where belief was not an afterthought but a guiding principle. Leaders set a tone that framed inclusion as essential rather than exceptional. Faculty development emphasized not only techniques but mindsets. Peer mentors were chosen not only for availability but for conviction. Belief became cultural, woven into the identity of the institution.

And when belief took root, the effects rippled outward. Students were more willing to advocate for themselves, peers began to see inclusion as natural, and institutions shifted from asking whether students with intellectual disabilities could succeed in college to recognizing that they were already succeeding.

Belief, then, is not a sentiment layered on top of policy and practice. It is the current that animates them, the force that transforms access into opportunity and opportunity into growth. Without it, systems can function but remain hollow. With it, higher education begins to reflect its truest purpose: to expand possibility for all who enter.

For me, this work has never been abstract. It has always carried Ella's face, her laughter, her stubbornness, and her determination. Every finding I've written about, I've watched play out in her life. I've seen what happens when they're missing, how exclusion feels when it's baked into the system, and how limited the horizon can look when doors are closed before a child even has the chance to try.

But I've also seen the opposite. I've seen her step into spaces where belonging was real, where her name was called with warmth, where her teachers and peers believed she had something to offer. I've seen what happens when systems are designed with her in mind, when resources are aligned and when belief isn't fragile but firm. In those moments, she doesn't just participate. She thrives. She begins to imagine herself differently, and we begin to imagine her future differently too.

That's why this chapter matters. Because it isn't only theory, and it isn't only her story. It's the recognition that higher education has the capacity to be something more, something truer to its promise. If institutions can build belonging, if they can create infrastructure that endures, if they can secure resources with vision, and if they can hold belief as the compass, then students like Ella will no longer be exceptions. They'll be the evidence of what was always possible, once the system dared to include them.

This is the journey of becoming. Not only hers, not only mine, but ours . It's a collective becoming that challenges us to reimagine higher education so it reflects the fullness of who we are and who we can be together.

I wouldn't call these themes the final word to any extent. They're more like markers on the path, reminders of where change has already begun to take hold. Belonging, infrastructure, resources, and belief all matter, but they're not everything. The real story is still being written, and we're part of that writing. What comes next depends on how willing we are to keep observing, keep questioning, and keep building alongside the students who are already showing us what's possible.

We're not working with abstractions anymore. The research is clear, the programs are real, and the outcomes are undeniable. Students with intellectual disabilities have shown us, again and again, that when they're given the chance, they rise to it. They don't just attend classes; they participate, contribute, and transform the communities around them. They remind us that inclusion isn't charity, and it isn't a gamble. It's a proven investment in human potential.

But evidence alone doesn't change the world. What changes the world is what we choose to do with it. The question now isn't whether students with intellectual disabilities can succeed in college. The question is whether we're ready to believe in them, ready to build for them, and ready to stop treating their presence as an exception.

That's the work that lies ahead. And that's where we turn next.

CHAPTER 13
THE MILES AHEAD

I can already see the morning unfolding. The light spills through the windows, steady and unhurried, filling the room with the sense that something important is about to begin. It traces the length of the hallway, warms the breakfast table, and pauses at the doorway as though holding space for what's to come.

Ella is dressed early. Her backpack leans against the door, upright and waiting, already filled with the things she's chosen to carry into this next chapter. Inside rests her iPad, the device that anchors her days, holding notes and playlists and sketches that track the rhythm of her life.

Her iPhone slips into the outer pocket, close enough for us to reach her and for her to reach us. Beside it rests a pen she chose simply because holding it made her feel like a student. From the zipper swings a small stuffed keychain, soft and familiar, the kind of reminder that brings a sense of home into new environments.

Her shirt catches the morning light. A shimmer that is part style and part declaration, her way of saying she belongs before she's even spoken. Her hair's tied just the way she likes it, brushed and smoothed until it matches the styling she had in mind. She pauses at the mirror, leans closer, makes one last adjustment, and smiles.

Her sister lingers nearby, careful not to hover. Advice comes in fragments, casual on the surface, but offered with care. Their rhythm is familiar and easy, a back and forth that belongs only to them. Sometimes it sounds like teasing, sometimes like guidance, but underneath is a tenderness that has always been there.

When we step outside, the air feels crisp, the kind of freshness that belongs only to the Fall and to new beginnings. In the car, music plays, conversation is limited, but laughter breaks out every so often as we recall the funniest moments from her childhood. A glance here, a smile there. Beneath it all is the reality of knowing this day has been years in the making. It's all so bittersweet because she's leaving home for the first time.

On campus, we fall into the current of families and students arriving with their own hopes and stories. Arrows point toward doors. The scrape of carts over pavement blends with the sound of greetings, laughter, voices calling out directions. And in the middle of it all is Ella. Her steps are even and her presence steady. She doesn't hesitate, but instead looks around curiously, looking for someone she might've known from orientation. This place was meant for her too.

At some point she glances at me, her voice calm and sure. "Look at me, Poppe. I'm living on my own now."

We move with the stream of families, carts rolling, suitcases stacked high, voices buzzing with pride and nerves. Banners hang from windows and balloons sway gently in the breeze, each detail arranged to mark the beginning of something important. Students rush past with arms linked, laughter trailing behind them. Parents linger close, caught between the urge to hold on and the quiet pull to let go.

The residence hall rises ahead with its doors wide open, framed by signs welcoming students to a new home. Inside, the air hums with motion. Elevators slide open and shut. Names are checked off with quick nods. Room numbers are handed out like invitations. Ella steps into it all with a confidence that feels natural, like it was always meant to be. She grips the handle of her rolling bag, moves forward without hesitation, and joins the flow of students with ease.

From down the hall, music drifts into the corridor. Doors swing open and close. Names are exchanged, new bonds beginning in the most ordinary of ways. The entire building feels alive, filled with the energy of people stepping into their own lives. And there's Ella standing confidently. She turns toward the window, and for a brief moment I see her reflection. It feels like I'm looking at both the young woman she already is and the one she's still becoming. She turns back with a smile that explains itself. It's her story unfolding in front of us.

Breakaway

I'm already teary-eyed just writing these words for the first time. On one hand, I can't wait for the day it finally arrives. On the other hand, I can barely imagine how difficult it'll be to let go, to watch my baby step into a world bigger than anything I can hold for her. I sure I won't keep it together because moments like this aren't meant to be neat or easy. They're meant to remind us how far love can stretch and how much courage it takes to go far in this world.

When that day comes, the tears won't just be about letting go. They'll be about everything it took to reach this moment. Every procedure, every appointment, every meeting that ended with more questions than answers. They'll be about the nights we wondered if the world would ever be ready for her, and the mornings when she showed us she was ready for the world. They'll be about the quiet strength she's carried into every space and the joy she's shared even when doors seemed closed.

This won't just be a goodbye. It'll be a celebration of a journey that's refused to be defined by limits. It'll be a reminder that the distance between what once felt impossible and what's now unfolding was bridged by love, persistence, and an unshakable belief in who she is.

So yes, I'll cry. I'll stumble over words. I'll hold her tighter than I should. But beneath all of that will be gratitude for the chance to see this day, for the honor of being her father, and for the hope that her future will shine even brighter than anything I can picture now.

The thing is, this moment isn't some distant dream. It's within reach, already beginning to take shape as barriers fall away one by one. Every conversation, every effort, every stereotype challenged has been laying the groundwork for success.

But mornings like this don't simply appear. They're built through persistence, through policies that carve out opportunities, through families around kitchen tables refusing to settle, and through educators daring to imagine more. They're also forged in research and inquiry, in nights spent with books scattered all around, in journal articles read and reread, in questions turned over until the outline of an answer comes into view.

That pursuit became the heart of my academic journey, as I set out to understand what it would take for higher education to fully welcome students with intellectual disabilities as participants in every sense. My evenings and weekends were spent on Zoom calls with professors and classmates as I traced one idea after another. There were times when family meals ended and I had to step away to meet a deadline, when weekends that might have been spent resting or exploring were instead consumed by writing and research, when my wife carried more of the household weight so I could press forward.

I learned to speak a new language, the language of research, and to practice a discipline that demanded patience, precision, and persistence. There were moments when exhaustion pressed in, when the house was still and I was the only one awake, but it was in those hours that I discovered how to imbue what lived in my heart into practical frameworks strong enough to stand on their own.

Out of that process, a picture began to take shape. It wasn't a checklist, nor was it a tidy set of solutions that could be copied from one campus to the next. It was something deeper, a pattern of themes that pointed toward the possibility of transformation. These weren't abstract ideas living only in theory. They were drawn from real lives, from students and families and educators already reshaping what higher education could look like.

Each theme became a marker on the path forward, a reminder that inclusion isn't about lowering expectations or making exceptions. It's about reimagining the system itself so that students like Ella step onto campus already knowing they belong, not because they fought their way in, but because the institution had prepared for their arrival.

What I hadn't expected when I began was how much the research would sharpen my view of Ella's journey. By day, I lived the reality of raising a daughter excluded from higher education's design. By night, I studied how exclusion becomes structure, how policies harden into culture, and how culture teaches itself not to question its own boundaries. That recognition changed everything.

It shifted me from being a parent wishing for change into a researcher determined to show that change was possible. Each interview, each theory, each pattern of data became more than an academic exercise. They became mirrors, reflecting Ella's story back to me and revealing that what seemed immovable was in fact constructed. And what has been constructed can always be made new.

There was so much clarity that came from holding the personal and the academic at the same time. The more I studied, the more I could see Ella's story reflected in the patterns of higher education, and the more I lived her story, the more urgent the research became. Each side sharpened the other until it no longer felt like two paths running parallel, but one journey unfolding in layers.

That recognition gave me more than perspective. It gave me resolve. I began to understand that the obstacles in Ella's way weren't fixed or immovable. They were decisions that had been made, systems that had been designed, and cultures that had been reinforced. And if they had been created, they could be created differently. That was the truth that carried me through the late nights, the long readings, and the endless revisions. It was never only about finishing a degree. It was about preparing to tell the story that had always been waiting to be told.

The morning I imagine for Ella, the shimmer in her shirt, the music in the car, the calm certainty in her step, isn't a dream. It is already reality in pockets of this country. Families are chasing it. Leaders are building it. Students are stepping into it with courage. What once felt distant is already close enough to touch.

The students are ready. The path is visible. The work ahead is ours. And here's the thing. This work doesn't belong only to program directors, professors, or parents like me. It belongs to anyone who cares about what education means, and what kind of future we want to hand to the next generation. You don't need a title or a budget line to be part of it. You only need to look at students with intellectual disabilities and see what has always been there: potential, curiosity, and the desire to belong.

Perhaps that means asking questions no one else thought to ask. Maybe it means standing beside a family searching for a place where their student can grow. Maybe it means rethinking the way you hire, the way you mentor, the way you build community. The gestures all matter.

The truth is, the most powerful changes don't come from big unveilings or press releases. They show up in ordinary moments when regular people choose to believe more is possible. They happen when someone not only opens a door, but makes sure that the space on the other side was built for everyone.

So let me say this as plainly as I can. The invitation is not to finish the work, but to join it. You don't need all the answers. You just need to keep asking better questions. You don't need permission. You can begin right where you are, with what you have, alongside the students who are already proving what is possible.

This is the work ahead. And it belongs to all of us.

CHAPTER 14
STEPPING FORWARD TOGETHER

From the first days in Pensacola, when a single word altered the shape of our lives, to the long nights in Birmingham where monitors and prayers kept us steady, to the fragile triumph of open heart surgery in Las Vegas, every stage asked something new of us. Each place marked us, each season revealed its own weight, and each time we learned how to keep moving forward with a kind of faith we had not known we possessed. Now, in Northern California, the landscape feels different, not because the challenges have vanished, but because the foundation beneath us has grown stronger. What once felt impossible has become the life we live each day, built with care and love.

As I look back across these years, I see more than trials survived. I see the texture of family life woven through every season. I see the way laughter found us again in ordinary moments, how the rhythm of school mornings and dinner tables steadied us when the future felt uncertain. I see Cady's presence growing beside her sister, giving Ella companionship and balance, reminding us that the life we were shaping could not belong to one child alone but to the whole family. Cady has taught us how to honor more than one dream at a time, to protect her freedom to flourish while celebrating her place in Ella's story.

Along the way we discovered that belief never grows alone. It gathers strength in the presence of others who are willing to see possibilities where others once saw limits. A physician who looked past a diagnosis and spoke of potential, a teacher who treated Ella as a learner before anything else, a peer who waved her into a circle of friends, a mentor who asked her opinion and waited for her answer. Each moment seemed small on its own, yet together they formed a rhythm that changed not only how Ella saw herself but also how we came to see what was possible for her future.

That rhythm extended beyond our family. It reached into classrooms where faculty chose patience over pity, into meetings where administrators began to listen with curiosity rather than doubt, into communities where families shared both their worries and their dreams. Little by little, what once felt impossible became a vision worth pursuing. The idea that higher education could welcome students with intellectual disabilities was no longer abstract. It was lived, it was studied, and it was carried forward by those who believed that belonging was not a favor to be granted but the true measure of education's purpose.

When I reflect on these years, I see more than progress in Ella alone. I see a community learning how to open itself wider, how to recognize that education at its best is not about protecting boundaries but about expanding them. My own work has been shaped by this truth. In classrooms, in interviews, in long evenings of writing and questioning, I searched for the patterns that turn inclusion from an idea into a practice. I noticed programs flourish when leadership was shared across roles, when advisors became companions, and when employers recognized strengths instead of limits. These were not theories to be debated. They were choices made daily by people who understood that belonging is the soil in which learning grows.

For me, this journey has been both personal and public. I have learned to speak when silence once seemed safer, to listen when answers came more slowly than I hoped, to gather people around a vision and keep them at the table long enough for change to take root. Leadership, I have come to believe, is not about holding authority but about holding trust. It's the patient work of carrying a vision forward, of keeping the door open long after the applause fades, of continuing to believe when others hesitate.

So when I stand in this moment and look at how far we've come, I don't see an ending. I see a foundation strong enough to hold the weight of what is still ahead. I see Ella stepping into the future with confidence in her voice and a presence that cannot be overlooked, and Cady flourishing in a life that is fully her own. I see a family that's chosen again and again to do the work of believing in public, and a community that now understands that inclusion is not an exception but the clearest expression of what education was always meant to be.

What we have built together is real. It lives in Ella's confidence, in the voices of families who now dare to hope, in the institutions that have begun to widen their doors. It lives in the doors once invisible, in the light revealed by hope, in the presence of students who now walk through spaces that were never designed with them in mind. And it carries with it the promise that this is only the beginning. Ahead lies a new chapter where possibility becomes practice, where a program welcomes Ella as a scholar, where belonging isn't conditional but assumed.

What I want to leave on these pages is something lasting. This journey's never just been about Ella or even about our family. It's always been about what can happen when enough of us choose to believe, when we keep doors open long after others have turned away, and when we hold tight to the truth that every student deserves a future worth building. That future isn't somewhere far off. It's here, alive in the choices we make each day, in the courage we show, in the spaces we dare to widen. And when we step forward, we don't do it alone. We step into the current together, carrying with us both the weight of what's been and the wonder of what's still to come. That's the work, and that's the hope, and that's the tomorrow already waiting for us.

EPILOGUE

Every story continues, even when we think the last chapter has already been written. Some carry forward in expected ways, steady and familiar, while others turn suddenly, surprising us with new beginnings where we thought there would be endings. Some stories move quietly, almost unnoticed, while others rise boldly, refusing to be ignored. Every story, no matter how it unfolds, holds within it the chance to reveal something more, a possibility we didn't see until the moment arrived. This is ours, still being written, still opening into possibility, still reminding us that endings are often just another way of naming beginnings.

And for us, the truth of that story shows itself most clearly in Ella and her sister, in the everyday moments that remind us where possibility lives.

Some mornings she sings before the day has even begun. Her voice drifts down the hallway, familiar melodies we know by heart because she plays them every day. They've become the soundtrack of our lives. Sometimes she hums softly to herself, other times she fills the house with joy, every note bold and unrestrained. I often stop just to listen. Her singing reminds me that the story doesn't live only in milestones or announcements but in the rhythm of ordinary mornings. It reminds me that hope isn't something distant. It's here, woven into the sound of a child singing her favorite songs without hesitation.

One day, she may step onto a college campus not as a visitor, not as a guest allowed a glimpse, but as a student. She may walk into classrooms where her name belongs on the roster, sit in spaces where she's expected, and learn among peers who know her not by a label but by her name. That chapter hasn't yet been written, but everything we've seen tells us it can be. What once felt improbable has already begun to show itself as possible.

I think back to an evening when Ella and Cady sat at the dining table, colored paper spread between them. Ella cut her shapes with care, pausing now and then to glance at her sister, who leaned in with the patience of someone who's always known she was both sister and teacher. When Ella lifted her finished piece high with pride, Cady clapped as if it were a masterpiece. In that moment, I saw the future in miniature: Ella taking her place with determination, Cady walking beside her with her own strength, both reminding me that inclusion begins at home.

But inclusion doesn't end at home. It grows in classrooms where teachers make space for possibility, in workplaces where talent is recognized before difference, and in communities where belonging is seen as essential. It expands when leaders choose patience over dismissal, when peers choose friendship over distance, and when systems are willing to bend toward something better.

What's been created so far is a foundation, but it's not enough on its own. The road ahead is long, and the work is unfinished. It's not just for Ella and her peers, but for all the families who wait for doors to open, for the schools and communities that don't yet know what they're missing.

Through years of study, conversations, and reflection, I've found the conviction to stay the course. I've seen what becomes possible when leadership is shared, when faculty lean in with patience, when advisors choose to walk alongside, when families are welcomed as partners, and when employers recognize ability instead of doubting it. These aren't ideals to admire from a distance. They're choices to live every day. And I intend to keep doing the work during the course of every conversation, in every partnership, and on behalf of every program still waiting to be built.

We can't rest because there's too much at stake. Families are waiting for someone to say yes. Students are waiting for a chance to stand in their own light. Communities are waiting for gifts they don't yet know how to receive. And yet I know this: change doesn't come in one sweeping act. It's built one day at a time. One classroom. One meeting. One moment of belief. Each day offers the chance to keep the vision alive, and each step, however small, carries us forward.

The story told here belongs to our family, but it's not ours alone. It belongs to the parents who lie awake wondering about the future of their child. It belongs to the teachers who pause long enough to see possibility where others only saw limits. It belongs to the administrators who choose to listen instead of dismiss, to the peers who wave someone in instead of walking past, to the leaders who refuse to treat inclusion as optional. Each of them holds a part of this story, and each of them has the power to write the next lines.

For me, this book has been more than a record of our family's experience. It's been a way of naming what's true. That belonging is possible, that belief can be lived out loud, and that hope endures as a force strong enough to build futures. It's been my way of declaring that the work ahead matters too much to leave unfinished, and my way of saying, with certainty, that I'm ready to keep doing that work.

The road ahead is long, but the doors are there to be opened. The light is present. The song is still being sung. Ella's voice is part of it now, steady and growing. Cady's voice too, rising with her own strength and her own future. Together they remind us that inclusion isn't only possible but necessary.

From that day in Pensacola when everything we knew changed, to this moment now, the truth has remained the same. Hope carries us forward. What comes next will be the measure of our legacy, calling us toward a future where every child has room to grow and flourish.

These are the miles we chase.

ACKNOWLEDGMENTS

This book began as one family's story, but it could never have been written without the love and strength of so many people who walked beside us.

To my wife, who's traveled this journey with me from the very first day, your faith has been the foundation of every step we've taken. To Ella, whose joy and determination inspire these pages, you've taught me more about resilience, love, and possibility than any classroom ever could. And to Cady, whose patience, laughter, and quiet strength remind me every day that inclusion begins at home, thank you for being both sister and teacher, for Ella and for me.

To my parents, who sacrificed more than words can capture, your journey from Vietnam to America made mine possible. The courage you carried across oceans is the same courage I try to live out for my daughters.

To the educators who believed in Ella, who saw her first as a student, thank you for opening doors when it would've been easier to leave them closed. To the families who shared their stories with me, in research and in friendship, thank you for trusting me with your hopes and your fears. Your voices echo throughout this book.

To my colleagues and mentors at USC, your guidance shaped the academic work that underpins these pages. You reminded me that scholarship matters most when it changes lives, and you pushed me to write with both precision and heart.

To the community leaders, advocates, and friends who keep showing up for students with disabilities in classrooms, workplaces, and neighborhoods, you prove every day that change is never the work of one person alone.

And finally, to every reader who turns these pages, thank you for carrying this story forward. It belongs to you now as much as it belongs to us. My hope is that something here moves you to believe, to act, and to reimagine what inclusion can mean in your own corner of the world. Together, may we keep chasing the miles ahead.

APPENDIX

A BRIEF HISTORY OF ACCESS TO INCLUSIVE POSTSECONDARY EDUCATION

This book is built on lived experience, but the story of inclusion stretches far beyond one family. The opportunities that exist for Ella, and for so many students like her, did not happen by chance. They were shaped by decades of advocacy, legislation, and research that slowly opened doors once thought permanently closed, and even now those doors do not stay open on their own. Every gain has been the result of struggle, persistence, and belief from those who refused to accept exclusion as the final word.

I've chosen to include this section, adapted directly from my doctoral dissertation, because history matters. To understand where we are today, and why access to higher education for students with intellectual disabilities is still fragile, we must first look back. This history explains how we arrived at this moment, why barriers remain despite the progress already made, and what must still be done to ensure that students with intellectual disabilities are not left waiting at the threshold of opportunity.

This is not simply a record of laws and policies. It's a record of choices, the ones that shaped the past, the ones we live with in the present, and the ones that will determine the future. By remembering how we got here, we begin to see more clearly the work still ahead.

Introduction

The World Health Organization defines individuals with intellectual disabilities (ID), including those with Down syndrome (DS), as having cognitive impairment that reduces their ability to understand new or complex concepts and to learn and apply new skills.[1,2] As these individuals mature and develop as members of a marginalized population, research indicates that while they desire postsecondary education, they inherently struggle with legal, financial, and institutional barriers, not to mention considerable academic obstacles.[3,4]

Despite a small number of laws helping increase the number of students with ID in postsecondary education, such as Section 504 of the Rehabilitation Act (1973) and the Individuals with Disabilities Education Act (IDEA), intellectually disabled students have continually shown the lowest rates of postsecondary enrollment among all disability groups.[5,6]

Although few statistics are gathered specifically for students with DS, the Centers for Disease Control and Prevention's (CDC) Behavioral Risk Factor Surveillance System (BRFSS) estimates that almost 30% of the U.S. population have a disability of some kind.[7,8] While precise numbers are blurred due to a fear of stigma and reprisal experienced by students with ID, recent data show a persistent gap in postsecondary institutions with only 21% of undergraduates and 11% of graduate students reporting a disability of some sort, whether physical, mental, or emotional.[9]

This continual lack of postsecondary education not only prevents students with ID from reaching their full academic potential but also gives way to an unemployment rate of 7.2%, which is more than twice the rate for those without a disability.[10] As a consequence, lower employment rates lead to greater disparities in support services, healthcare, housing, and inclusion, making postsecondary education a crucial problem to address, imbued with issues of access, inclusion, accountability, and advocacy.[6]

Background of the Problem

Access to limited postsecondary programs is still the most formidable barrier for students with ID in higher education.[11] Historically, the United States has offered postsecondary education only to those with a high school diploma and satisfactory progress toward academic benchmarks, thereby excluding students with ID who were deemed unable to participate in the academic and social rigors of college life.[12] Legislation on behalf of students with ID goes back nearly five decades with the signing of Section 504 of the Rehabilitation Act (1973). Often referred to as "Section 504," it became one of the very first civil rights laws enacted to protect students with ID by specifically prohibiting discrimination against individuals with disabilities from participating in programs funded by the federal government, including public schools and postsecondary institutions.[13]

Subsequently, Section 504 became the precursor to formative civil rights legislation in the Americans with Disabilities Act (ADA) (1990), which provided individuals with disabilities equal opportunities for participation in programs and activities in all areas of public life.[14] As part of this landmark legislation, the ADA specifically demanded that institutions of higher education provide reasonable modifications on behalf of students with ID, and in conjunction with Section 504, both laws work to protect students with ID from being discriminated against based on their disability.[11] [13]

Specific initiatives to include students with ID in postsecondary programs are rooted in the reauthorization and renaming of the Education for All Handicapped Children Act (1975) to the Individuals with Disabilities Education Act (IDEA) in 1990. IDEA focused on six pillars for students with ID and recognized that all students with disabilities had rights to free and appropriate public education in the least restrictive learning environment.[12] While IDEA only applies to primary and secondary school settings, it marked a new era in special education by giving advocates, parents, and students with ID a new framework through which to view their path toward postsecondary education. Most notably, and in contrast to the civil rights legislation presented in Section 504 and ADA which pushed for students with ID to have the same experiences as everyone else, the language behind IDEA demanded that the educational programs be differentiated and customized to be effective, depending on the needs of the student.[15]

Described by researchers as a demographic storm, the decline of college-age students in the United States has created many challenges for the nearly 4,000 institutions of higher learning nationwide.[16] With weakening revenue streams due to decreased student enrollment, there exists institutional concern that increased operational costs will prompt campus closures, especially among small liberal arts colleges serving the middle class.[17] Whether or not these campuses eventually close, a full assessment of challenges to enrollment patterns, retention rates, degree and course offerings, and overall expenses will be required for most institutions.[18]

The fact that postsecondary education is increasingly desired by students with ID underpins the importance of understanding how these programs operate and succeed despite institutional attempts to reduce funding and resolve operational deficits.[19] As more college-age students with ID transition out of high school with a desire for future employment, considered the cornerstone of a successful segue into adulthood, it is critical to examine and share the strategies inherent to successful postsecondary programs for students with ID.[20]

Failure to internalize key considerations, particularly for students with ID, will prevent the development of a clear vision as institutions individually address common barriers.[18] Inversely, to achieve a shared vision, geographically separated institutions should collectively leverage best practices to resolve complications ranging from financial support and funding to the accessibility of modified coursework, and faculty willingness to teach intellectually disabled students.[21]

Historical & Legislative Context

The historical and legislative context surrounding postsecondary education for students with ID has developed incrementally over multiple decades, with pivotal legislation increasing access and equity. Critical legal milestones, including Section 504 of the Rehabilitation Act, the Americans with Disabilities Act, the Individuals with Disabilities Education Act, and the Higher Education Opportunity Act, have each contributed to expanding educational rights and accommodations for students with ID.[22] Each of these laws have established foundational steps for students with ID through their unique provisions and each have also faced challenges in implementation.[23]

Section 504 of the Rehabilitation Act (1973)

Enacted over 50 years ago, Section 504 of the Rehabilitation Act has played a fundamental role in protecting persons with disabilities from discrimination. Working alongside subsequent legislation, namely the Americans with Disabilities Act (ADA) and the Individuals with Disabilities Education Act (IDEA), Section 504 establishes Free Appropriate Public Education (FAPE) in the form of equality and accessibility, thereby addressing barriers toward postsecondary education for students with ID.[22]

Section 504 also signified a turning point in attitudes toward disability rights in the United States, leading a transition from perceiving disabilities as medical impairments to examining disabilities within a civil rights context.[24] Most notably, and in contrast to other mandates that promote individualized progress and student-specific outcomes, Section 504 frames disability rights through an outward-looking equity lens, requiring that students with ID learn in educational environments comparable to those of their neurotypical peers.[25]This protection is distinct because it extends beyond the K–12 classroom, offering support for students with ID should they transition to postsecondary programs regardless of age.

Despite its extended scope, educational institutions and courts have historically encountered challenges in interpreting and implementing Section 504 accommodations, leading to inconsistent legislative support for students with ID. This inconsistency poses continual barriers for both advocates and students, as they battle against ableist attitudes, undermining beliefs, and institutionalized biases that reduce the effectiveness of well-intentioned legislation.[26]

To address these limitations, more rigorous evaluation and research are needed to assess whether Section 504 accommodations in postsecondary education are creating equitable environments and producing intended outcomes versus simply facilitating basic access requirements.[26] For students with ID, these limitations underscore the importance of working toward evidence-based interventions to develop strategies that actively promote workforce skill development, social inclusion, and independent living instead of deploying modifications to solely satisfy the legislative requirements of Section 504.[27]

While Section 504 is considered a legislative anomaly because of the relatively small amount of public attention it received upon its enactment, it has nevertheless served as one of the first civil rights laws enacted to protect people with disabilities from discrimination.[24] In the coming years, as more postsecondary programs are developed for students with ID, additional research is required to further analyze the impact of Section 504 accommodations and evolve from simply offering accessible learning environments to establishing true education equity.[26 22 25] In conjunction with more contemporary laws such as the Americans with Disabilities Act, Section 504 will remain relevant legislation, providing a basis of protection for students with ID in postsecondary education.

Americans with Disabilities Act (1990)

The Americans with Disabilities Act also serves as foundational civil rights legislation, intended to protect individuals with disabilities from discrimination in both public and private spaces. Within the context of higher education, the ADA is noteworthy due to its broad scope and the intention to secure equal opportunities for students with disabilities by ensuring accessible campus facilities, educational materials, and digital resources.[28] Since its enactment in 1990, the ADA's protections have intertwined with those of Section 504, ratified almost two decades prior and designed to prohibit federally funded institutions from excluding students with ID from their programs.[22]

Research has underscored the importance of reasonable accommodations under the ADA, which include technological learning aids and services that facilitate participation for students with ID. Despite a heightened demand for digital tools, along with an increased awareness of accessibility challenges faced by students with ID, many institutions have been slow to adopt, failing to execute upon the ADA's commitment to equitable learning environments.[29] Additionally, the ADA has been shown to adversely affect postsecondary achievement for students with ID as data indicate that in U.S. states lacking prior disability protections, the ADA's implementation coincided with a decrease in educational attainment among students with ID.[30]

While the ADA intended to provide equal access and prevent discrimination for students with ID, its effectiveness was limited until the passage of the ADA Amendments Act (ADAAA) in 2008. Before the amendments, the ADA's strict definition of disability and the documentation requirements were barriers to receiving both proper student services and specific workplace accommodations.[31] The ADAAA expanded the definition of disability, broadening protections for more students with ID while reframing the documentation's purpose from proving that disabilities exist to evaluating whether functional limitations are preventing learning.[31] This paradigm shift required institutions of higher learning to implement new policies and procedures to accommodate broader legal standards, especially as it pertained to determining eligibility and providing accommodations to students with ID.

Individuals with Disabilities Education Act (1990)

The Individuals with Disabilities Education Act, first passed in 1990, was a reauthorization of the Education for All Handicapped Children Act (1975). The primary aim of IDEA was to expand educational opportunities for students with ID, ensuring them a Free Appropriate Public Education (FAPE).[32] In contrast to Section 504 and the ADA, the IDEA focused on a different aspect of FAPE, looking inward and expanding educational access by mandating individualized support for students with ID to progress in their education.

The Individualized Education Program (IEP) serves as the foundation for a student's FAPE, documenting each student's specific needs and goals in an effort to enable meaningful progress. Developing the IEP is a collaborative effort involving school personnel and parents, blending the expertise of educators with the insight of the child's family.[23]

However, while IEPs are still written and updated across the board for students with ID, there are barriers to their execution as funding challenges and human costs continue to exist. In fact, the Supreme Court has reinforced that while the IDEA promotes educational progress, it does not ensure proficiency, inherently recognizing schools' limited resources as a limitation.[32]

Most relevant to postsecondary education for students with ID are the 1997 amendments to the IDEA, which strengthened transition planning for students exiting the high school environment.[32] Similar to the IDEA's FAPE guidelines, these updated provisions required transition services tailored to each student's needs, interests, and goals, emphasizing self-determination as essential to successful postsecondary progress toward employment and independent living skills.[33] In support of these IDEA amendments, research has shown that students with ID who received interventions that enhanced self-involvement and empowerment showed significant improvements over time, and promoting student involvement has become a best practice in educating students with ID.[33]

As with previous legislation, while the IDEA has achieved progress in ensuring educational access and equity, ongoing challenges remain. Financial and human resources continue to constrain IEP implementation in schools, and further advocacy is still needed for special education as a distinct and specialized support system tailored to students with ID.[32] [23] However, in looking toward the future, there are still foundational benefits to leverage, such as Part D of the IDEA, a rarely mentioned program. Part D programs, while undeveloped as a small fraction of IDEA's funding, bridge research and practice and have been pivotal in advancing early intervention, assistive technology, and behavior management for students with ID.[23]

Higher Education Opportunity Act (2008)

Efforts to increase educational access for students with ID have gradually evolved over the years, shaped by additional legislation intended to further the mission. The Higher Education Opportunity Act was a legislative milestone that introduced provisions to expand postsecondary education access and inclusion for students with ID.[34] Through establishing guidelines for the creation of Comprehensive Transition and Postsecondary (CTP) programs, including the Transition and Postsecondary Programs for Students with Intellectual Disabilities (TPSID), the HEOA opened pathways for students with ID to participate in more inclusive learning environments alongside their peers.[34] Furthermore, HEOA legislation expanded access for students without traditional high school diplomas, addressing a longstanding barrier for students with ID attempting to transition from secondary to postsecondary programs.[35]

The HEOA legislation aligns with IDEA (2004) guidelines, advancing the intent to provide comprehensive support systems for students with ID and creating deeper relationships between higher education institutions and the surrounding community.[36] However, inconsistent program designs and eligibility criteria have impeded evidence-based practices, preventing the fulfillment and implementation of the HEOA's inclusive goals.[37] Further research is crucial to evaluate the HEOA's impact on course accessibility, student progress, and the effectiveness of accommodations in academic environments.[37]

Given the increased integration of technology in modern learning environments, a mentality of lifelong learning is essential for all students, and especially for students with ID. Effective implementation of the HEOA will depend on collaborative efforts extending beyond higher education itself, including Local Education Agencies (LEAs), Developmental Disability Authorities (DDAs), and Vocational Rehabilitation (VR) services to provide support during the transition from high school.[36] The alignment of resources and expertise is essential as each of these systems, in conjunction with legislation such as the HEOA, lends distinctive practices, policies, and methods to support inclusive outcomes for students with ID in postsecondary education. Through these efforts, institutions can create universally designed programs that not only meet the HEOA's mandates but also evolve inclusive educational experiences for all students.[37]

Significance of this Work

Described by researchers as a demographic storm, the decline of college-age students in the United States has created many challenges for the nearly 4,000 institutions of higher learning nationwide.[38] With weakening revenue streams due to decreased student enrollment, there exists institutional concern that increased operational costs will prompt campus closures, especially among small liberal arts colleges serving the middle class.[39] Whether or not these campuses eventually close, a full assessment of challenges to enrollment patterns, retention rates, degree and course offerings, and overall expenses will be required for most institutions.[40]

The fact that postsecondary education is increasingly desired by students with ID underpins the importance of understanding how these programs operate and succeed despite institutional attempts to reduce funding and resolve operational deficits.[41] As more college-age students with ID transition out of high school with a desire for future employment, considered the cornerstone of a successful segue into adulthood, it is critical to examine and share the strategies inherent to successful postsecondary programs for students with ID.[42] Failure to internalize key considerations, particularly for students with ID, will prevent the development of a clear vision as institutions individually address common barriers.[40] Inversely, to achieve a shared vision, geographically separated institutions should collectively leverage best practices to resolve complications ranging from financial support and funding to the accessibility of modified coursework, and faculty willingness to teach intellectually disabled students.[43]

The history and context outlined here remind us that progress is never automatic. It's always been built step by step, law by law, and choice by choice. Each piece of legislation, each ruling, and each act of advocacy widened the path for students with intellectual disabilities, yet none of it guaranteed the future. These gains remain fragile unless they are carried forward in classrooms, on campuses, and in communities that choose to live them out every day.

The demographic challenges ahead and the institutional pressures of higher education make this work more urgent, not less. For families like ours, these laws and policies are not abstractions. In fact, they shape the daily realities of our children's futures. They determine whether Ella will be seen first as a student, whether her peers will know her by her presence instead of her diagnosis, and whether communities will recognize her contributions as necessary to their wholeness.

But as this book has shown, history alone is not enough. Laws open doors, but it's people who keep them open. The next chapter of inclusion will be written not just in legislation, but in the collective choices of educators, leaders, families, and students who believe that belonging is not optional, but essential.

What comes next depends on us.

ENDNOTES

APPENDIX

1. Cluley, V. (2018).
2. Potier, R., & Reeves, M. (2017).
3. Barron, D. (1999).
4. Yssel, N., et al. (2016).
5. Grigal, M., & Papay, C. (2018).
6. Lehrer-Stein, L., & Berger, M. (2023).
7. Centers for Disease Control and Prevention (CDC). (2024). *Disability datasets.*
8. Loveall, S. J., et al. (2022).
9. Digest of Education Statistics (2023). Lehrer-Stein, L., & Berger, M. (2023).
10. U.S. Bureau of Labor Statistics (2024).
11. Lehrer-Stein, L., & Berger, M. (2023).
12. Vinosky, T. D., Thomas, J., & Carter, E. W. (2020).
13. Murphy, J. (2020).
14. Americans with Disabilities Act of 1990, Pub. L. No. 101-336.
15. Lemons, C., et al. (2024).
16. National Center for Education Statistics (2024).
17. Adamiec, T., et al. (2022); Biemiller, L. (2015).
18. Zemsky, R. (2020).
19. Pavlov, O., & Katsamakas, E. (2020); Sheppard-Jones, K., et al. (2015).
20. Loveall, S. J., et al. (2022).
21. Plotner, A. J., & Marshall, K. J. (2015).
22. Raj, A. (2021).
23. Yell, M. L., & Bradley, M. W. (2024).
24. Chamusco, C. (2017).
25. Schraven, J., & Jolly, J. (2010).
26. Mitra, S., & Turk, M. (2024).
27. Hustus, C., et al. (2020).
28. Garcia-Torres, A., et al. (2024); Koen, D. (2017).
29. Garcia-Torres, A., et al. (2023).
30. Reinarts, J., & Melo, L. (2023).

31. Keenan, W. R., et al. (2019); Koen, D. (2017).
32. Rooney, P. (2018).
33. Seong, Y., et al. (2015); Yell, M. L., & Bradley, M. W. (2021).
34. Madaus, J. W., et al. (2012); Talapatra, D., & Snider, M. (2022).
35. Grigal, M., & Papay, C. (2018); Madaus, J. W., et al. (2012).
36. Butler, R., et al. (2016); Talapatra, D., & Snider, M. (2022).
37. Becht, K., et al. (2020); Talapatra, D., & Snider, M. (2022).
38. National Center for Education Statistics (2024).
39. Adamiec, T., et al. (2022); Biemiller, L. (2015).
40. Zemsky, R. (2020).
41. Pavlov, O., & Katsamakas, E. (2020); Sheppard-Jones, K., et al. (2015).
42. Loveall, S. J., et al. (2022).
43. Plotner, A. J., & Marshall, K. J. (2015).

ABOUT THE AUTHOR

Loc H. Nguyen is an Air Force veteran, educator, nonprofit leader, and doctoral candidate at the University of Southern California. As founder of the BTR TMRW Center for Advancement, he works to expand postsecondary opportunities for students with intellectual disabilities. His first book, *The Miles We Chase*, weaves personal story with advocacy for systemic change in inclusive post-secondary education.

in linkedin.com/in/lhnguyen2

www.ingramcontent.com/pod-product-compliance
Lightning Source LLC
Chambersburg PA
CBHW031505120626
46545CB00005B/1754
9798218780883